WHEN ONLY *Faith* REMAINS

FINDING YOURSELF *in the*
Life of Mary,
the MOTHER *of* JESUS

WHEN ONLY _Faith_ REMAINS

FINDING YOURSELF _in the_
Life of Mary,
the MOTHER _of_ JESUS

AMY C. O'REILLY

Published by Redemption Press, PO Box 427, Enumclaw, WA 98022
Toll-Free (844) 2REDEEM (273-3336)

Redemption Press is honored to present this title in partnership with the author. The views expressed or implied in this work are those of the author. Redemption Press provides our imprint seal representing design excellence, creative content and high quality production.

Unless otherwise noted, all Scriptures are taken from the Holy Bible, New International Version®, NIV®. Copyright © 1973, 1978, 1984, 2011 by Biblica, Inc.™ Used by permission of Zondervan. All rights reserved worldwide. www.zondervan.com.

Scripture quotations marked "ESV" are taken from The Holy Bible: English Standard Version, copyright © 2001, Wheaton: Good News Publishers. Used by permission. All rights reserved.

Scripture references marked TMB are taken from The Message Bible © 1993 by Eugene N. Peterson, NavPress, POB 35001, Colorado Springs, CO 80935, 4th printing in USA 1994. Published in association with the literary agency—Aline Comm. POB 49068, Colorado Springs, CO 80949. Used by permission.

Scripture references marked NLT are taken from the Holy Bible, New Living Translation, copyright © 1996, 2004 by Tyndale Charitable Trust. Used by permission of Tyndale House Publishers, Wheaton, Illinois 60189. All rights reserved.

Scripture quotations marked HCSB have been taken from the Holman Christian Standard Bible* Copyright@1999, 2000, 2001, 2002 by Holman Bible Publishers. Used by permission.

Scripture references marked NASB are taken from the New American Standard Bible, © 1960, 1963, 1968, 1971, 1972, 1973, 1975, 1977 by The Lockman Foundation. Used by permission.

ISBN 13: 978-1-68314-713-8
ePub ISBN: 978-1-68314-714-5
Kindle ISBN: 978-1-68314-715-2

Library of Congress Catalog Card Number: 2019930785

Table of Contents

Pondering Sacred Echoes

But Mary treasured up all these things, pondering
them in her heart.

—Luke 2:19

What does it mean to ponder something at the heart level? The dictionary says to ponder is to think about something carefully, to consider, to meditate, or to reflect, especially before we make a decision or reach a conclusion. While we may start to ponder in the mind, what does our pondering look like when it moves from the head to the heart? In Luke 2 we find what Margaret Feinberg recently called a "sacred echo," where Mary, the mother of Jesus, "ponders" and "treasures" certain events in the life of Jesus at the heart level. Following the birth of Jesus and a visit by the shepherds, "Mary treasured up all these things and pondered them in her heart" (Lk. 2:19). We don't have to read much further to discover what reads like literary déjà vu in Luke 2:51: "But his mother treasured all these things in her heart." These two verses read like a divine echo, reverberating from ancient words regarding sacred moments within a mother's heart.

For several years I have pondered these verses, which led me to write about Mary's journey of faith—from God calling Mary to bear His Son, to her witnessing His crucifixion, and beyond. Perhaps, in pondering the words spoken about her Son Jesus, Mary ultimately found and came to know her Savior. Perhaps it is through pondering God and His Word that we find and come to know Jesus as our personal Savior.

As I followed Mary's journey in Scripture, God began to reveal many parallels in my own life and faith journey. While battling an eating disorder, anxiety, depression, and tragedy in my life, I found connection and hope in Mary's journey with Jesus to the cross. Initially, through these sacred echoes, I sensed God calling me deeper into His Word, into the heart and mind of Mary, into a deeper knowledge of Him, and into a journey of faith like I had never before experienced. God showed me just how far He has carried me into a place of healing and completeness.

You see, I am just a Bible study girl who loves to read about Jesus, talk about Jesus, and teach about Jesus. Just give me Jesus! That's my humble equivalent of Paul's proclamation in 1 Corinthians 2:1–2: "When I came to you, I did not come with eloquence or human wisdom as I proclaimed to you the testimony about God. For I resolved to know nothing while I was with you except Jesus Christ and him crucified." Through my study of Scripture in relation to Mary's life, God has relentlessly pursued me, because He understands my desire to relate to a real person. Because God knows we all need real people and stories that are like our own to cling to for hope and inspiration when life unravels, He gave us people like Mary.

As I read through Luke 2, I often wondered what Mary was pondering. As she held her firstborn baby, what was she *really* thinking? Was she just riding on post-labor emotions and hormones, trying to make some sense of this much-anticipated moment in time? Or was she meditating on a deeper truth, one that God had begun to reveal to her since her encounter with the angel Gabriel? In Luke 2:51, as we hear a sacred echo of Mary treasuring all those things in her heart . . . *heart* . . . *heart*, we see God pierce Mary's heart in merciful preparation for events to come. I have to admit, I was both intrigued and terrified to dig deeper. What was Mary *really* thinking? What was God *really* doing in her life? Just as the famous song inquires, we have to wonder, "Mary, did you know?"

As I pondered Mary in my own heart, I discovered Mary's story is every believer's story; your religious affiliation does not matter. Mary's story is that of every mother and every woman who is brave enough to say yes to Christ and yes to the life He wills for her. Believers as a whole, especially women, can identify with and relate to Mary as they begin to understand the complexity of her calling.

Mary's story is heartrending, yet beautiful, and crushing, yet full of hope, and it's replete with anticipation, insecurity, fears, doubts, grief, hope and love. Her story is one of mystery and intrigue. It is also sobering with a heavy dose of the realities involved in following Christ. And hidden just beneath the surface of Mary's unique calling to serve as the mother of Christ lies an equally captivating story of her journey of faith. From the first time she says yes to Jesus in the presence of an angel to the day she is filled once again with the Spirit of her risen Savior at Pentecost, we witness a frightened Jewish girl transformed into a woman who overcomes the worst grief imaginable—all by faith.

Mary is the paramount example of a faith flourishing in the midst of all of life's emotions, confusion, shattered dreams, and dreams come true. Her faith is there on the pages of Scripture for us to relate to, connect with, and receive the true gospel message. As I dug past the details and circumstances of Mary's life to unearth her core needs, fears, and desires, I found myself identifying with Mary more and more. I discovered God at work in each detail of her life and in every relationship, teaching her His ways and deepening her faith, just as He has done in my life. In Philippians

2:12, Mary is the perfect example of a believer who "works out her salvation with fear and trembling," as God teaches her to trust His plan through the life and death of her very own Son. Thus Mary's journey of faith becomes one in which all roads lead her back to Jesus, the Christ, the Lord and Savior of all.

Come with me on this journey as I share my own life experiences in light of Mary's journey as found in Scripture. My hope is that Mary becomes real and relevant to you in a very personal way throughout the pages of this book. My prayer is that, as you find yourself and your own journey of faith in the story of Mary, your faith in Jesus Christ will be renewed and strengthened. During the times in our own lives when only faith remains, we can look to Mary's faith and truly find hope in trusting Jesus, the founder and perfecter of our faith (Heb. 12:2).

CHAPTER ONE

Faith, Hope, and Love

And now these three remain: faith, hope, and love.
But the greatest of these is love.

—*1 Corinthians 13:13*

What do you do, and to whom do you turn, when life gets hard and downright hideous, when all love seems lost, and when hope doesn't float anymore? What do you do, and to whom do you turn, when love has abandoned you and glimmers of hope are unrecognizable from the depths of the pit where you stand broken and contrite? I have experienced such depths of this pit, the most dangerous place on earth, and have had to face those same difficult questions.

I was thirteen years old when I developed bulimia, and I was caught in the abyss between all-consuming fear and blind faith in the dark depths of my own personal hell. In my experience, bulimia was a manifestation of a deeper disorder of my heart and soul, fueled by a need to control, to be perfect, and to perform my way through family, school, and athletics.

As a child of divorce, with both parents remarried, I grew up in two amicable homes. But the wounds of divorce—the constant coming and going from each parent's house and the periods of isolation from either Mom or Dad—had taken their toll during the crucial, formative years of adolescent development. Soon, to keep the peace between four parents and to feel wanted and loved, I became a parent-pleaser. While I matured physically and mentally, my emotional health suffered. Before long I found it hard to cope with the normal stress of day-to-day life. Eventually, my spirit crumbled under the mounting, self-inflicted pressure of producing, performing, and coveting praise.

From my teen years well into my twenties, I secretly turned to food for comfort. Food seemed to fill the void caused by always feeling like I had failed God, my parents, and myself. I relied on food to fill the emptiness and pain in my soul, despite all the success, grades, and accolades I had achieved along the way. As a competitive runner with seriously low body fat, I turned to rich, sugary foods for comfort and relief. To avoid the consequences of the sin of overeating, I made myself sick, but the resulting rush of emotional and spiritual guilt and shame was often overwhelming.

During those frustrating and confusing teen years, my journal entries read, "I'm sorry, God. I messed up again. I promise to try harder tomorrow. I promise to do better." I constantly felt like I was disappointing either God or my parents, teachers, and coaches, because I was hiding my pain behind an embarrassing secret. I thought I had to be smart enough and strong enough to get better on my own, so I wouldn't upset my parents and expose my fragile emotional state. The effort to press on in my own strength, while enduring such a physically, mentally, and emotionally damaging disorder, was exhausting.

A concerned coach came right out and asked me, "Are you anorexic?" I confidently replied, "No!" He'd seen the pain in my tired eyes, but he just hadn't asked the right question.

My unhealthy and dysfunctional relationship with food continued for fifteen years, despite professional counseling, family support (after eventually telling my parents), and medical treatment. I tried to keep my bulimia a secret. My mask of perfectionism and work ethic usually hid my feelings of insecurity and inadequacy. The dysfunctional thinking and hypocrisy that accompany bulimia bled into other areas of my life. After a career-ending running injury in my college years, life as I knew it—along with every significant relationship—spiraled down the drain of depression, isolation, and hopelessness. I came to a dead end in a dark corner where it felt as if bulimia had won. I remember thinking, *This is it. This is who I am. I will never get better. This is most likely how my life will end.* I felt helpless, powerless, and weak, dangling over a grand canyon of hopelessness. I was ready to let go, or so I feared.

When I was about ten, I had accepted Jesus Christ as my Savior, but I did not understand how faith can build a bridge between insecurities and God. I often wondered: if what Scripture says is true, that "these three remain: faith, hope, and love," then why didn't it always *feel* this way? Why are our choices in life so often reduced to somewhere between fear and faith, not love, hope and happily ever after? My days were filled with doubt, and there were times when life felt pointless because I didn't understand Who I was living for. When I reached the point where I had lost all hope and hardened myself against any outpouring of love, I had to hold on for dear life, because that was the point when only faith remained.

Have you ever experienced a time when it felt like only faith remained? When faith is your last hope of ever experiencing the love of God, don't give up. Hold fast to faith. What do you do, and to whom do you turn, when your only remaining choice is somewhere between fear and faith? Whether we are in the deepest pit or experiencing the highest mountaintop, we've all faced this predicament and made a decision at some point in our lives. Do we choose fear or faith, self-doubt or self-surrender? Do we run and hide from God like Adam and Eve, or can we find the faith to stare headlong into the face of something greater than ourselves?

Mary, the mother of Jesus, understood this feeling, this life-changing, pivotal choice, this predicament of providential proportions! And Mary has a lot to teach us about those moments in life when only faith remains. Although our historical knowledge of Mary is limited, she is woven into Scripture in ways that reveal many truths about God, about Christ, about the power of the Holy Spirit, and about how God used her most important relationships in life for His glory. God utilized everything in Mary's life to teach her about Himself. From the moment she was born, she had a calling, whether she realized it or not. In His perfect timing God poured His Spirit over Mary so that His will would be done on earth, as it is in heaven. God introduced Mary to her Savior in the most intimate way, forming first an umbilical cord in the living bond between mother and child, and later forming a relationship that would eventually become her own eternal lifeline.

God has also placed a calling on each of our lives. In fact, I keep a little Willow Wood plaque of Mary and Joseph on my bookshelf all year round. It reminds me of God's calling on my life to teach and write about Him and His Word. Our calling may seem trivial compared to Mary's; however, to compare them is to miss the point completely. The point is *how* God teaches us, not *what* He uses. God uses our individual calling to teach us His ways, His character, His mercy, and His great love for us. God's greatest desire is for us to know Him, and, while the teaching is the same, the journeys to knowledge and understanding are different. Even Mary needed to learn about unconditional love and unwavering hope, so God took her on a journey to the cross. He does the same for us. We can learn so much from studying Mary and all the places she appears in Scripture because ultimately God is trying to teach us some of the very same truths.

God's calling on your life and mine doesn't necessarily include a divine pregnancy, but it does include an invitation to enter into an intimate relationship with Jesus that permeates the deepest and most delicate parts of our being. Similar to what Mary experienced, God utilizes everything in our lives to draw us closer to Him. He uses our strengths, our weaknesses, our friends, our spouse, our worst nightmares, and our highest hopes to reveal His great love, grace, and mercy. Let us celebrate Mary's journey, knowing God has each of us on a journey of faith, salvation, and completeness in Christ.

As the mother of Jesus, Mary is revered by many. However, our love for Mary as the mother of Christ unites us in a passion for learning about and exploring her journey of faith. We find common ground in God's grace and admire His work in Mary's life and faith. Let us all unite in the essentials of our Christian faith, for we are all God's people, the church, and the body of Christ here on earth. May our personal theology not place boundaries around our personal transformation.

Take a moment to think about where you are on your journey. Maybe you have yet to meet your Savior, or maybe you've been on your journey of faith with Christ for many years. Perhaps your life's journey has taken you places you never really wanted to go or given you experiences you only wish you could forget. It's okay. You are never too far from God for Him to lose sight of your soul. He sees you, He seeks you, and He sent His Son to rescue you from sin. When God calls us into His will and purpose, He sovereignly orchestrates each page of our story—each leg of the trip, each season, each detour, each pit stop, and each seemingly dead end—to somehow lead us back to Him. He uses everything and wastes nothing. Let us follow Mary to the cross and beyond, no matter what the cost, trusting that all roads will lead us back to Jesus, the author and finisher of our faith.

PRAYER

God, broaden and deepen our walk of faith as we embark on this journey with Mary. By the power of the Holy Spirit, open our hearts and minds to Your will and Your way. Help us to identify with, relate to, endear, embrace, and fall in love with Mary, the mother of Jesus, as we grow closer in faith and love to the Father and the Son. In Jesus's name. Amen.

CHAPTER TWO

Engaging in the Unexpected

"For I know the plans I have for you," declares the Lord, "plans to prosper you and not to harm you, plans to give you a hope and a future."

—Jeremiah 29:11

Getting engaged is one of the most exciting and memorable moments of a woman's life. Most girls dream of finding a husband to provide, protect, and love her just the way she is—fearfully and wonderfully made, yet perfectly imperfect.

My own engagement did not disappoint. My boyfriend, much to my surprise, proposed to me on Labor Day weekend at my childhood summer home. Although my parents were away camping, they had invited us and another couple to enjoy the last days of summer at their log cabin on the lake, fully equipped with a hot tub and ski boat. The lake was one of my favorite places on earth, filled with memories of sunrise skiing on glassy water, catching and cleaning fish to fry, sailing, and watching fireworks on the Fourth of July from the boat. I loved the sun-kissed skin, sunsets from the pier, and sleepovers on the screened-in porch. Lake life was the only life I had known as a child. I spent many nights hypnotized by the moonlight reflecting on the rippling water, dreaming of the future and a special someone with whom I might share moments like these.

My boyfriend knew this place held special meaning, so he carefully planned his proposal to create a lasting memory for me and my family. After he popped the question in his own signature way, I melted in the surprise of it all and couldn't wait to go tell our friends, who of course knew it was coming! And then I called my parents, my sisters, my brother—anybody who would answer their phones—because I could not release the excitement fast enough. I beamed for days, stared at my engagement ring every thirty seconds, and fiddled with this new sensation on my ring finger. For weeks following the proposal, I tried to allow the reality that *I was engaged* to sink into my being. The fact that *he* asked *me* to marry him was all I could see as I watched that circular piece of love on my finger sparkle in the sunlight.

A few days after our engagement, I celebrated my birthday with my parents and his, and we began to talk about wedding plans. It was an incredibly full week, yet nothing could stop me from daydreaming about what our wedding day would be like and who would attend. What kind of wedding dress, flowers, music, and food did I want? Where would we honeymoon? The mental to-do list went on and on! I was on cloud nine, and my dreams of having a family of my own were starting to fall into place. My heart was full of love, and my future full of hope.

I floated on that cloud for a few more days until the morning of September 11, 2001. Suddenly all that was right in my happy world silenced when two planes crashed into the World Trade Center twin towers, an historical event now referred to as 9/11. Although we were physically far removed from the tragedies of that day, my future husband had family in New York, including police officers and firemen who responded to the call. I had an aunt who often worked at the Pentagon. The frantic calls began, first to my fiancée, then to my parents. Do you know anything? Have you heard from anyone? Are they okay? No one could get through, and so for hours we waited—America waited—trying to work and trying to hide the sheer panic in our hearts from what we had witnessed on television that morning.

Days later, when we had heard from everyone, we were relieved. Yet many of them had lost friends, partners, and fellow officers. Relief turned to mourning as our family and our country mourned. I found myself feeling guilty even thinking about my wedding for weeks and months following 9/11. My future plans felt as if a dimmer switch had been activated, and darkness surrounded us more than light.

In Scripture, one bride's plans to wed were temporarily derailed for a season. Mary was betrothed to Joseph, a carpenter from Nazareth. We are first introduced to the youthful couple in Matthew chapter 1, where the emphasis is placed on Joseph. We learn of Joseph's all-important lineage and his noble character as a righteous man. We also get a glimpse of the tug-of-war between his heart and his mind as he ponders the news of his fiancée's alleged infidelity. Later, in Luke chapter 1, the story is told from Mary's perspective.

Let's consider the scene of their engagement and the glorious days that would have followed such a happy announcement. The Bible doesn't tell us much about their time together before Gabriel announced the life-altering news, but we women can surely speculate what Mary was thinking and anticipating during her engagement to a man from the line of David. Joseph was from a good family, a good pedigree. He had a job, he was a well-respected, faithful, and righteous man. Best of all, he loved Mary and wanted to honor her in all things. Perhaps for Mary, Joseph was faith, hope, and love—all wrapped up into a carpenter from Nazareth.

During biblical times, an engagement or betrothal signified a legally binding commitment between a man and a woman, as well as their families, dissolvable only by divorce. Culturally, an engage-

ment was a solid commitment between two hearts, not to be broken by the shifting sands of life, circumstances, or family drama.
Mary was committed to Joseph, and Joseph to Mary.

I can only imagine how excited they were to announce the
news to their respective families and begin planning their future
nuptials. Joseph probably carved Mary's name into every piece of
scrap wood in his shop, and Mary probably took the long way to
market to buy grain, just to pass by Joseph's house. I wonder how
many stolen moments they found together as they anticipated the
day the two would become one in holy matrimony? Perhaps Mary
felt butterflies as she watched Joseph refine his craft and stand at
the city gate, an honored and well-respected man. And Joseph may
have gazed upon Mary, a faithful and humble Jewish maiden, with
tender eyes. Mary's future was full of hope. Her dream of having a
family of her own was starting to fall into place until the unexpected happened.

In Luke chapter 1 we read about Mary's encounter with the
angel Gabriel, which leaves her bewildered and uncertain of her future. Perhaps Mary is gazing out her window, neglecting her chores
for a moment, daydreaming about Joseph. Out of the blue, Gabriel
appears, startling her from a preoccupied stare into an apprehen-
sive stance. Luke 1:28–38 captures this life-altering moment:

> The angel went to her and said, "Greetings, you who are
> highly favored! The Lord is with you." Mary was greatly
> troubled at his words and wondered what kind of greet-
> ing this might be. But the angel said to her, "Do not be
> afraid, Mary; you have found favor with God. You will
> conceive and give birth to a son, and you are to call him
> Jesus. He will be great and will be called the Son of the
> Most High. The Lord God will give him the throne of his
> father David, and he will reign over Jacob's descendants
> forever; his kingdom will never end." "How will this be,"

Mary asked the angel, "since I am a virgin?" The angel answered, "The Holy Spirit will come on you, and the power of the Most High will overshadow you. So the holy one to be born will be called the Son of God. Even Elizabeth your relative is going to have a child in her old age, and she who was said to be unable to conceive is in her sixth month. For no word from God will ever fail." "I am the Lord's servant," Mary answered. "May your word to me be fulfilled." Then the angel left her.

The biblical text seems to move so quickly to Mary's obedience, that we must intentionally pause to consider her possible thoughts and emotions. Within these first moments of shock and awe, having heard she was favored and blessed and chosen to carry the Messiah, perhaps she felt the tug in her heart because of her pledge to Joseph. The love and hope she shared with Joseph were suddenly in jeopardy. "How can this be," she asked, "since I am a virgin?" She not only had trouble understanding physically how this could happen, she also couldn't comprehend exactly how these two worlds could collide. Mary was puzzled and caught off guard. Perhaps she squirmed and wanted to resist and give excuses about why this wasn't a good idea, but she didn't.

Although her dream of an ideal union with Joseph was temporarily blemished, she no doubt contemplated what this all would mean to her life, her family, and her dreams. Perhaps in her heart she said yes to her God but in her mind was afraid of the consequences of obedience. In the moment when she encountered the love of God through the voice of an angel, it was her faith that said yes, despite the consequences. In a moment when her feelings of love and hope for Joseph seemed threatened, it was her faith in God that remained. In these moments when only faith remains, we, too, are forced to ask the confusing questions.

These verses show us that when life is going along just fine, then the unexpected happens, our first priority must be to trust God with the outcome. Perhaps in that moment Mary didn't fully comprehend everything the angel spoke regarding Jesus. Even if she was familiar with the prophecies of Isaiah and Zechariah, and God's promise to send a Savior-King to His people, did this prepare her for the presence of an angel, the overshadowing of the Holy Spirit, and the calling of a lifetime? Mary had much to lose because her love for Joseph was so great. However, she had much more to gain by trusting God's plan for her life. "For I know the plans I have for you," declares the Lord, "plans to prosper you and not to harm you, plans to give you hope and a future" (Jer. 29:11). Had Mary ever heard of this verse, and did she understand it as a promise from God?

We claim God's promises by faith because He is able to do immeasurably more than anything we could ask or imagine, according to His power that is at work within us (Eph. 3:20). Faith can start like a mustard seed—the smallest seed on the planet—yet when planted, it grows and becomes the largest of all garden plants (Mk. 4:30–32). Little did Mary know what plans God had for her, plans to prosper her and not to harm her, plans to give her a future and a hope—a future that still included Joseph. Although the angel spoke of His greatness and the kingdom to come, little did Mary know the power that was at work in her very womb. In those moments when Mary was face to face with Gabriel, God's messenger, she chose by faith to trust God with her future, and ultimately Joseph's future. When the unexpected happened, she surrendered to the loss or pain she might incur and chose instead to place her reverence for God above the unknown.

God is always in the unexpected. Just expect it! He always shows up in the most unlikely circumstances in ways we can't even anticipate. Mary never could have imagined the plans God had for her: she would become a mother before she was a wife; she would give birth to the Savior of the world; and she would have the family she'd always dreamed of in a most unusual way.

I can so relate. My husband and I were married in May 2002, and we had our firstborn child that same year. Not the way you want to start a marriage—pregnant and hormonal. But His ways are not our ways, and sometimes He lets us have our own way, so He can show us The Way. Though my first pregnancy was unexpected, God was faithful to work all things for His good in my life. But more on that in a later chapter.

My experience of 9/11 pales in comparison to those who lost loved ones on that tragic day, but the questions that followed apply to anyone who has ever encountered the unexpected. Where do you go when the unexpected happens? What do you do when your plans don't line up with God's plans? To whom do you turn when you enter into the unknown? These are questions we all will face one day if we haven't already. The losses our country faced on 9/11 reminded us all that nothing in life is guaranteed, and ultimately we are not in control. "'For my thoughts are not your thoughts, neither are your ways my ways,' declares the Lord" (Isa. 55:8). "The heart of man plans his way, but the Lord establishes his steps" (Prov. 16:9 ESV).

I had big plans. I had a wedding to plan and a future to behold when the unexpected happened and snuffed the eager anticipation of this bride, but only for a season. Joseph and Mary were the ideal couple, busy planning their ideal life, when the unexpected showed up. Have you ever been there? Busy living your life, with close family, supportive friends, acceptance to a great college, a good job, a faithful boyfriend or husband, a healthy child, or certain expectations of the future—and then the unanticipated and uninvited barges through the door? Your parents get a divorce, one of your friends starts a nasty rumor on social media, college applications become overwhelming, you lose your job, your boyfriend cheats, your child is diagnosed with a life-altering illness, or you endure the frustration of a series of unmet expectations. Suddenly without warning, a good life can be reduced to uncertainty and bewilderment at best.

Your disappointment or tragedy may look like an obstacle, a predicament, a detour, a force to be reckoned with, or even a dead end, but it just might be God trying to get your attention, hoping you will surrender to His plan. However this looks in your life, I pray you can relate to Mary's fears of losing control and begin to discover God's sovereign hand upon you in a very real way.

In her book *Unexpected*, Christine Caine writes, "We cannot shrink back in fear and go forward in faith at the same time." Although Mary was afraid, fear did not stop her from asking questions. Faith alone allowed her to move closer toward the will of God. Every unexpected moment in our life is an opportunity to exercise faith.

PRAYER

Lord, help us acknowledge fear and uncertainty in the unexpected and exercise faith by trusting in You and Your unfolding plan. Like Mary, help us move closer to the center of Your will, even when it's not the way we expected. In Jesus's name. Amen.

CHAPTER THREE

A Life-Changing Yes

Behold, I am the servant of the Lord; let it be to me
according to your word.

—Luke 1:38 ESV

I was about ten years old the very first time I said yes to Jesus. A friend had invited me to attend a Christian summer camp in the North Carolina mountains. Despite nervous butterflies (it was one of my first times being apart from my parents for more than a few days), I packed my bags, loaded them on the bus, and bravely waved goodbye as I rode off to an adventure of a lifetime.

Camp was the most fun I'd ever had. Days were full of swimming, archery, water skiing, making pottery, and playing soccer. Swimming in warm lake water surrounded by lush green mountains felt like a great big hug from God. You could almost taste the sweet smell of honeysuckle in the breeze. But what I remember most are the evenings gathered around an outdoor firepit, smelling the burning wood and roasting marshmallows as the counselors led us in worship songs about Jesus. I can still feel the cool night breeze against my back and the fire's warmth in front while I worshiped Jesus, arms outstretched, experiencing His loving presence for the very first time. I didn't know many of the songs at first, but by the end of the week I couldn't get those Spirit-filled songs out of my head or my heart.

One night, while a teary-eyed counselor shared her story about accepting Jesus as her Savior, the Holy Spirit came over me and filled me, much like those camp songs had filled my heart. In that moment I knew I wanted to RSVP the invitation being offered by the One who died on the cross for me. Overcome with emotion and tears myself, for the first time that week I didn't care what anyone else thought about me. I was experiencing the call to salvation and eternal life, and my answer was a confident yes. During that week, I realized for the very first time that I needed something greater than myself to become the person I was called to be and that something was being offered in the Person of Jesus Christ. I knew I needed Jesus, but little did I know the pit from which He would one day raise me and the journey of faith He would lead me through.

We all have different faith journeys, yet the invitation is offered out of the same great need for a Savior. Ever since man's fall from grace in the Garden of Eden, God knew the only way to restore the untainted relationship he shared with the first man and woman would be through the sacrificial life and death of His Son. Jesus's life and death were foretold by the Old Testament prophets, but no one could have predicted the time or the place the Savior would arrive—not even Mary.

As far as we know, Mary was going about her normal day, performing the mundane tasks of a maiden's life, when a vision and a voice appeared in the form of an angel. Many scholars believe Mary was in her early teen years when Gabriel announced her chosen destiny. At an age when most girls are searching for their identity, Mary discovered her destiny. As we read through Gabriel's message in Luke chapter 1, we discover many truths about God and His plan for the redemption of not only Mary, but all of humanity.

Gabriel approached Mary saying, "Greetings, you who are highly favored! The Lord is with you." Speaking through His messenger Gabriel, the heavenly Father greets Mary right where she is, in the midst of her life and her circumstances. This is an important detail to point out, because we often think of people in the Bible as being well prepared for an encounter with God. We assume that people like Abraham, Moses, Daniel, Queen Esther, and David had their life together when God called them to join Him in His kingdom work. As children we are taught all the familiar Bible stories on a level of understanding appropriate for a child, but the Sunday school version of these stories reveals neither the depravity and ineptitude of each of these individuals nor their ultimate dependency upon God.

As far as we know, nothing prepared Mary for her introduction to the Father, Son, and Holy Spirit. She was going about her life the best she knew how, dreaming, hoping, longing, perhaps struggling at times, but pressing on toward her future with Joseph. Whatever condition she was in that day, God showed up in Mary's life at just the right time, because God's timing is always perfect.

Gabriel's salutaion, "Greetings," let Mary know she was being approached as a friend, by a friend, for friendship's sake. When God greets us, He comes as a friend who promises to stick closer than a brother (Prov. 24:18). Gabriel spoke the favor of God over Mary, assuring her that she was in the very presence of the Lord. Initially, these words were overwhelming and even troubling to Mary. God speaking directly to her through an angel was a foreign concept to Mary. She had probably only experienced God through stories told in her Jewish home and community, or through Scriptures and prayers recited by rabbis in the local center of worship. Understandably, her mind was trying to catch up with the reality of what Gabriel was speaking into her heart.

Perhaps Mary was deeply troubled following these first few words of greeting. As her anxious thoughts gave way to fear, what God did next reveals so much about His character and His great love for His children. Only God knows the heart of a man or woman. He had Gabriel speak intimately into her heart, validating her emotions. "Do not be afraid." Then he called her by name. Gabriel did the talking, but it was God speaking those words of affirmation and love into Mary's heart. He acknowledged her fear and her perplexing thoughts, and with the love and compassion of a Father, he called her by name, claiming her as His own. The phrase "do not be afraid" occurs over seventy times in the NIV, more than any other command in the Bible. God understood the paralyzing effects of fear. He knew that hearing her name, Mary would then be able to hear and receive the life-changing words that followed.

After speaking these intimate words of comfort to Mary, Gabriel repeated the phrase "You have found favor with God," thereby emphasizing God's amazing grace as the forerunner to Mary's chosen status and her calling. It was only by God's grace that any of this happened. By God's grace He chose Mary. By God's grace He called Mary to be the mother of Jesus. By God's grace He sent Gabriel to deliver an intimate and personal message to her. By God's grace, the Holy Spirit came over Mary, allayed her fears, conceived the life of Christ, and entrusted her with the privilege and responsibility of being the mother of the Messiah.

Not one day of Mary's calling was lived apart from the grace of God, because it was birthed out of the love of God. Just as the power of the Holy Spirit conceived life in Mary, the love of God gave grace and favor and enabled Mary's rebirth in the Spirit. Mary was blessed and favored because God loved her. After experiencing the love and grace of God in a personal way, Mary was ready to hear the plans God had for her life.

The next few words spoken by Gabriel encapsulate Mary's calling: "You will conceive and give birth to a son, and you are to call him Jesus." Seated in the heart of Gabriel's message are life-changing words. In this unexpected event, the point at which Mary would never look back, the very will and purpose of God for her life was revealed. If we read these verses too quickly, we will miss it, because the following verses are all about Jesus. In fact, I wonder if Mary heard anything past, "You will conceive and give birth to a son." Judging from her response, it's likely that this is where her mind got stuck . . . conceive . . . give birth . . . a son.

"How will this be," Mary asked the angel, "since I am a virgin?" Several Bible commentaries agree that this was not a question born out of disbelief. This was simply an attempt to understand. As Mary first heard the words of her calling spoken by an angel, she questioned the miracle it would require.

Perhaps Mary could not comprehend *how* God was going to take her from her current circumstance and condition into the center of His will. Had she fully comprehended what Gabriel explained to her that day, she would have immediately understood how. "You are to call him Jesus. He will be great and will be called the Son of the Most High. The Lord God will give him the throne of his father David, and he will reign over Jacob's descendants forever; his kingdom will never end" (Lk. 1:31–33).

The name Jesus (Joshua in Hebrew) means "the Lord is salvation." Had Mary fully comprehended the significance of Gabriel's news, that she was to give birth to the One whom the prophets foretold as the Messiah, the One who came to reconcile all mankind back to its Maker, the Savior-King, the Shepherd-Servant, the tender shoot from Isaiah, she would not have needed to ask how. But Mary didn't know; she couldn't fully comprehend the significance of the One she was to call Jesus. So she asked the question we all must ask when we discover the gulf between our present reality and the life God calls us to: "How will this be?" In Luke 1:35–38 we find her answer:

The angel answered, "The Holy Spirit will come on you, and the power of the Most High will overshadow you. . . . So the holy one to be born will be called the Son of God." "I am the Lord's servant," Mary answered. "May your word to me be fulfilled." Then the angel left her.

Once again, we see a glimpse of the character of God as Gabriel answered Mary's question of how. God, in His sovereignty and omniscience, doesn't owe us any explanations. As our Creator and Sustainer, He doesn't have to reveal to us why or how. In fact, the answers to these types of questions usually contain some of the mystery of God. God didn't have to tell Mary how, but in His great love and compassion He revealed to her the mystery of His Holy Spirit. By graciously answering Mary's request for understanding, God made known to her the presence and power of His Spirit. Mary had just been introduced to the Trinity.

That day the angel Gabriel revealed to Mary one of the greatest mysteries of the gospel. The power and presence of the Trinity became the "Holy One" in her womb, the very Son of God. When God places a calling on our lives, He may not always reveal *how* He will accomplish it. *How* is usually a long process of trust and transformation, with a prerequisite of faith. But even though God doesn't always answer how or why, at least not immediately, He wants us to continue to ask. Like Mary, He wants us to continue to seek understanding in hopes that we will find and know Him more intimately.

Mary's last words before the angel departed were, "May your word to me be fulfilled." This is Mary's yes to Jesus. A life-changing yes. In these moments, Mary laid down her life, her plans, and her dreams, and she submitted to the will of God. Little did she know that God's Word to her included the fulfillment of God's plan since the beginning of time. God's Word was not only life-changing for Mary, but it is life-changing for us too! As we embrace the love of

God and He meets us where we are, He will begin to reveal His calling and our destiny. Through the power of the Holy Spirit we will begin a journey of faith that, like Mary's, leads us to the cross and beyond.

During her encounter with Gabriel, Mary realized for the very first time that she needed something greater than herself to become the person she was called to be, and it was being offered in Jesus, the One who saves. Maybe she thought Jesus needed her as a mother, and maybe she knew she needed Jesus as a Savior, but little did she know the journey of faith she was about to begin. The Holy One in her womb would soon transform her into a woman of God, blessed among women, because of her faith and her unique calling as the mother of Jesus.

Mary had a choice: to live inside the will of God or to run and hide like Adam and Eve and bring Joseph into hiding with her. Thus, her decision was a life-changing yes, both for her and for Joseph. When we have the courage to say yes to Jesus and yes to the will of God in our lives, we are ultimately blessing all the other relationships in our lives with God's love, acceptance, and grace.

Maybe you've been there? Maybe you have stood in Mary's sandals, wondering how your newfound relationship with Christ will affect all your other relationships? It's a glorious, yet unsettling place to be. Glorious because the angels are rejoicing at your acceptance into the kingdom and unsettling because of your ties to those who may not understand or accept your decision. It's important for us to know, and in this case to learn from Mary, that our acceptance of Jesus is really more about His acceptance of us. When we come to the place of humility, where we find the end of ourselves and our own inability to manage and cope with life, that is where we run headlong into the love and acceptance of God. His will for our lives is ultimately about knowing, loving, and serving Him, and thus, glorifying Him in the process.

When God speaks to us today through the Holy Spirit, our experience may seem similar to Mary's. It can feel like something overtakes us. Our pulse increases, our heart begins to pound, and thoughts and ideas not our own are spoken in our minds and hearts, though not always audibly. It's the same sensation I experienced at ten years old when I lifted my arms in worship and accepted Jesus as my Savior, and it's the same feeling I've had many times when God was calling me to speak to a stranger or a room full of people in His name. God speaking or nudging us through the Holy Spirit can seem troubling, almost scary. This experience usually calls us out of our comfort zone, and it's hard to obey and trust. Rest assured though, when God reveals Himself to you, He comes as a friend. His very presence is overflowing with grace and favor.

Do you remember the first time you said yes to Jesus? Maybe you remember the exact day and time, or maybe you have a more general sense of your acceptance of His love and saving grace over time. If you've never accepted His invitation of unconditional love, salvation, and eternal life, it's okay. Please keep reading. It's better for you to understand what that really means, than to accept it out of blind fear or dismiss the invitation altogether. I believe that not until we experience the love of God in a personal way, can we begin to discern His will and purpose for our lives. Apart from the love of God, we are more likely to lean on our own understanding, focus on our own dreams, and try to satisfy our own desires. However, when we've been touched personally by the love of God, we are more likely to say yes to Jesus. A life-changing yes will lead us into the will of God, the only place where our deepest longings are satisfied.

Jesus is the personification of God's unconditional love. He is the One who was, and is, and is to come. He is the One by whom all things hold together, and for whom all things were created, and live, and breathe, and have their being. But God knows that just as Mary couldn't comprehend her calling to carry the Messiah in her womb, we can't comprehend the significance of the life and death of Christ until we've traveled down the road that leads to the cross.

Our invitation to accept Jesus as the One who saves is usually met with the same uncertainty. Perhaps we are told as children that He is the One who saves us from our sin, He is God's Son, and the Lord of all, and we can live forever with Him because His kingdom has no end. Perhaps as adults we take it a step further and we understand that Jesus fulfilled prophecy, He is omnipotent, He reigns at the right hand of God Almighty, Satan is His footstool, and His will shall be done on earth as it is in heaven. But how does Jesus affect us, change us, and lead us into our calling in the center of God's will? Like Mary, we have to be willing to start down the road that leads to the cross. Like Mary, we have to be willing to ask the confusing questions. And like Mary, we can't allow our fear to overcome our faith.

As the angel departed, Mary was left with two destinies, her own and her child's. As the fruit of her womb grew, never had two destinies intertwined in such a way for God's glory. One destiny led to death on the cross so that the other's destiny would lead to life everlasting. Mary is blessed and greatly loved among women and men, because she teaches us that we are all destined to meet and come to know our Savior.

2 Corinthians 1:20 (NLT) says, "For all of God's promises have been fulfilled in Christ with a resounding Yes! And through Christ, our Amen (which means yes) ascends to God for his glory." Mary's willingness to submit to the will of God allowed the promises of God to be fulfilled in Christ to the glory of God. Like Mary, when we say yes by faith in Christ, He will fill our innermost being with His Spirit and lead us down the path of the promises of God.

In the moment when Mary feared losing Joseph's love and her future with him, it was her faith in God that prevailed, as she said yes to Jesus for the very first time. When God's love or someone else's love feels distant, and hope seems like a vapor, just remember that faith is not a feeling. Faith is a Person, and you (insert your name) are to call Him Jesus.

PRAYER

Dear Lord, help us arrive at the place of faith where we too, like Mary, can say, "Behold, I am the servant of the Lord; let it be to me according to your word." May Jesus be our life-changing yes. In His sweet name. Amen.

Chapter Four

Breath of Heaven Friendship

*When Elizabeth heard Mary's greeting, the baby
leaved in her womb, and Elizabeth was filled with
the Holy Spirit.*

—Luke 1:41

Who is the first person you pick up the phone and call when something wonderful happens or something terrible happens? If you had asked me that question several years ago, I would have said my mom. She was my solid rock during my childhood and well into my twenties and early thirties. I grew up much like an only child, in a very extended family with a half-brother whom I saw every other week and stepsisters who came to stay in the summer. I had lots of friends growing up but functioned very much as a loner, with a quiet, yet fiercely independent spirit. Once I got married and survived the adjustment period of "leave and cleave," which took me several years, my husband slowly became my closest confidant and the first one I called when I had news to share. Today, by the grace of God, I can thankfully say my husband is my very best friend. We share our best and worst moments—and everything in between.

I still have a strong relationship with my mother and a blessing for a husband, but friendships with other girls and women have always been a struggle. As a child I craved a soul connection with another girl who would play Barbies, talk about boys, and share each other's diaries. But that one friend always seemed to either elude me or turn on me. Living with a secret eating disorder made it harder for me to form attachments with people, including my parents at times. I could never allow anyone to get too close, for fear of them figuring out I wasn't who they thought I was. Believing the lie that bulimia defined me, I felt like a fraud and a hypocrite, but my heart still craved what my mind most feared—true friendship and full exposure.

God knows the desires of our heart. He planted them there for us to experience meaningful relationships, not only with parents, spouses and our children, but also with girlfriends. At thirty-something, after sabotaging potentially meaningful relationships and repeatedly failing miserably as a friend due to fear and shame, I began to pray for a godly girlfriend. As Jesus read the longings of my heart, He knew I desired the companionship of another mature Christian woman with whom I could talk, relate, laugh, cry, pray, and do life with. God had brought me to a place where I could finally learn what it meant to be a true friend and in turn receive love from an unconditional friend. As God often does, He answered my prayer in the most unlikely way. God gave me not one, but two Jesus-loving friends. Once our paths crossed, we quickly became best friends for life and sisters in Christ. We are like a beautifully braided cord, interwoven through the ups and downs of life. Although not always on the exact same path, we can quickly and easily reconnect as we journey the same direction toward Christ and His calling on each of our lives.

After Mary's encounter with Gabriel, God also knew the desire and subsequent quaking of Mary's heart. In Luke 1:36 Gabriel tells

Mary her relative Elizabeth is in her sixth month of pregnancy. Elizabeth, once barren, was experiencing firsthand the faithfulness of God. And Gabriel adds that "no word of God will ever fail." Nothing is impossible with God, because His Word will not return to Him void. Little does Mary yet know that this Word of God is the fulfillment of prophecy in Elizabeth's baby, John the Baptist, the forerunner to Christ. Gabriel's revelation of Elizabeth's condition is no coincidence. It is the providence of God.

When Mary came unexpectedly face to face with her destiny, she turned to Elizabeth, not Joseph. I'm convinced this was why, in the midst of Mary's calling, Gabriel shared with her the news about Elizabeth's pregnancy. God knew Mary needed a confidant—a faithful servant of God with whom she could talk, laugh, cry and pray, and most importantly, someone she could trust. In the hours and days that followed this life-altering event, Mary needed someone to run to, and given the circumstances, she wasn't prepared for that someone to be Joseph. Luke 1:39–45 tells the story:

> At that time Mary got ready and hurried to a town in the hill country of Judea, where she entered Zechariah's home and greeted Elizabeth. When Elizabeth heard Mary's greeting, the baby leaped in her womb, and Elizabeth was filled with the Holy Spirit. In a loud voice she exclaimed: "Blessed are you among women, and blessed is the child you will bear! But why am I so favored, that the mother of my Lord should come to me? As soon as the sound of your greeting reached my ears, the baby in my womb leaped for joy. Blessed is she who has believed that the Lord would fulfill his promises to her!"

In the days following God's revelation of His plan for Mary, Scripture doesn't say that Mary contacted Joseph. No, not at all. How could she? Perhaps the thought of having to tell Joseph that she was pregnant, and then to explain how, was too overwhelming.

Would he ever believe her? Mary still couldn't believe it herself. She couldn't comprehend the miracle that had just taken place, nor could she believe her own response in faith. Bewildered and afraid, Mary hurried to see Elizabeth. There is no way of knowing whether "Elizabeth, your relative" means that Elizabeth was Mary's aunt or cousin, but one thing is for sure—Mary needed a girlfriend to talk with! Can you relate? It's no coincidence that Gabriel mentions Elizabeth's name and her condition, because Elizabeth was exactly who Mary needed in this season of life. Mary needed the life-giving words of a friend.

Why not Joseph? Why didn't Mary go running to her beloved after hearing such wonderful, frightening news about the next nine months and beyond? The answer to this question lies in her response to Gabriel. "I am the Lord's servant," Mary said. "May your word to me be fulfilled." Mary said yes to Jesus, both literally welcoming Him into her womb and spiritually welcoming Him into her heart. Before she said yes, she established both her position as a servant of God and His priority in her life. Why didn't she go running to Joseph? After confessing God as her Master and the Lord of her life, she didn't yet know how this life-changing decision would affect her relationship with Joseph. Mary was unsure and perhaps afraid to find out. Fortunately for Mary, God would soon provide the answer.

Who knows what was going through Mary's mind as she hurried from Nazareth to Judea? I can envision Mary giving one courtesy knock on the door before bursting into Elizabeth's home with every emotion on the spectrum of feelings. Scripture says that, upon the sound of Mary's greeting, the baby inside Elizabeth's womb leaped with joy, and Elizabeth was filled with the Holy Spirit. Mary didn't get a word in edgewise as Elizabeth exclaimed, "You are the most blessed of women, and your child will be blessed!" When the Breath of Heaven entered the room, the Spirit of Heaven moved the heart of Elizabeth toward adoration and praise, showing that nothing we think we can say or do in a moment of crisis can compete with the power of the Holy Spirit's interceding.

Elizabeth explained to Mary that she was overwhelmed with the knowledge of being in the presence of the mother of her Lord—the Savior Himself, based on the reaction of the child in her own womb. The baby (John), being filled with the Holy Spirit, fulfilled Gabriel's prediction to Zechariah (Luke 1:15). Then, with Mary's greeting as the catalyst, Elizabeth was filled with the Spirit, and divine revelations were apparently the source of her knowledge about the blessed roles and identities of Mary and her unborn child.

Just as Mary arrived with a heart full of wonder, yet fearing that she had lost all hope for a future with Joseph, Elizabeth affirmed Mary's decision of saying yes to God and yes to His will in her life. Through the discernment and inspiration of the Holy Spirit, Elizabeth validated Mary's faith when she said, "Blessed is she who has believed that the Lord would fulfill his promises to her!" Elizabeth's proclamation not only validated Mary's faith, it also restored hope in Mary's heart about her future. Elizabeth's words helped Mary embrace the reality of her sacred calling, while reminding Mary of God's great love for His chosen ones. Just as Abraham believed and his faith was credited to him as righteousness, Mary also believed and received her Savior. Therefore, God both humbled and exalted her as a blessing for all women of all time.

Like best friends who hadn't seen one another for ages, Elizabeth and Mary reconnected instantly as two soul sisters, joined by the Spirit of God. Having a friend who can peer into your heart through the look in your eyes and speak words of promise and affirmation is truly a blessing from above. God knew exactly what and who Mary needed after the most important decision of her life. He knew she needed someone who could identify with her circumstances, relate to her emotions, and help elevate her faith above her fears by reminding her of the promises of God.

Psalm 37:4 (ESV) says, "Delight yourself in the Lord and he will give you the desires of your heart." Elizabeth gave Mary permission to delight herself in the Lord and trust in the promises of God—for her life, her baby's life, and Joseph's life as well. A true friend will always point you back to God, and that's exactly what Elizabeth did for her beloved friend. Elizabeth helped Mary see that her life was about to become all about Jesus, and she could trust God with the rest of her story.

Little did I know, when I met Jesus as a child at Christian summer camp, that I had met a Friend who sticks closer than a brother or a sister. I had made a Friend for life, who would not come down and play Barbies with me or read diaries out loud, but would read the inner longings of my heart. God created us for relationship, to build bonds, and to connect souls, with the Trinity serving as our ultimate model. He gave us the heart desire for human companionship, connection, and friendship.

My adult friends' prayers on my behalf have served as a lifeline during difficult times in my marriage and with my children. Like the relationship between Mary and Elizabeth, these women understand my struggles because they experience similar difficulties and hardships. We can share openly and honestly through a bond of love and trust. I have also prayed for these women very difficult prayers that God's will be done, even if the outcome resulted in somehow compromising the friendship. James 5:16 (NLT) is a wonderful reminder of how God works through faithful friends: "Confess your sins to each other and pray for each other so that you may be healed. The earnest prayer of a righteous person has great power and produces wonderful results."

As women, we need faith-filled girlfriends like Elizabeth who will steer us back to God. Girlfriends who, when we enter the room with our heads hung low, will remind us that God is the "lifter of my head" (Ps. 3:3). Girlfriends who will only allow us to wallow in our troubles for a moment, then speak life-giving words of hope and truth into our trials and tribulations. Girlfriends who will get on their knees in prayer on our behalf despite the bumps, bruises, or broken nails it may require. Girlfriends who believe in the Breath of Heaven, Jesus Christ, as the source of all wisdom and truth in a world that doesn't usually make sense. We all need women in our lives who will befriend the Holy Spirit before befriending you and me. We all need an Elizabeth, and we need to rely on the Holy Spirit in order to *become* an Elizabeth.

Men need true friends, too. In Scripture the close friendship between David and Jonathan parallels the friendship between Mary and Elizabeth. David and Jonathan shared a covenant friendship. 1 Samuel 18:1 (ESV) says, "The soul of Jonathan was knit to the soul of David." Men and women alike have been given the gift of relational living through the Spirit of Christ, and we all long for a heart and soul connection with a friend. While the dynamics of men's friendships may look different than women's friendships, God is always glorified when we point each another in brotherly or sisterly love back to Him.

Women, who is your Elizabeth? And men, who is your Jonathan? If you don't have a woman or man like this in your life, a sister or brother in Christ with whom you can bear your soul, I encourage you to delight yourself in the Lord, and He will give you the desire of your heart. He created you for relationship, and He who promised is faithful and able to fill that longing in your heart for deep connection with another godly woman or man. Start praying today for God to bring someone into your life or to reveal a friend who is already there. I found my best friends at my son's preschool and at church, in God's perfect timing and perfect way. And when you find them, it will feel like the Breath of Heaven blowing encouragement and hope into the empty spaces of your heart.

PRAYER

Dear God, thank You for the friend we have in Jesus and the model of relationship You provide within the Trinity. Help us form bonds of love and trust with other faith-filled friends who will steer us back to You and Your promises. Through the power of your Holy Spirit, may we be the Breath of Heaven to those we befriend, love, and serve. In Jesus's name. Amen.

CHAPTER FIVE

A New Hope, a New Song

*He put a new song in my mouth, a hymn of praise to
our God. Many will see and fear the Lord and put
their trust in him.*

—Psalm 40:3

As a junior in high school, I became the 800-meter state champion runner, set school and conference records in multiple track events, and began to receive recruitment offers from several Division I colleges. At the beginning of my senior year, I officially committed to my lifelong dream college. At seventeen I looked forward to pushing myself even harder to run faster times and establish myself as a serious contender in the world of NCAA track.

Then, during the spring track season, I landed wrong after clearing a hurdle and partially tore my Achilles tendon. Proverbs 16:9 (NLT) says, "We can make our plans, but the Lord determines our steps." I can still remember the burning twinge in my left heel and the subsequent dagger of fear that struck my heart. This was my first major injury—a significant setback followed by months of rehab. My physical limp was coupled with a crippled spirit, and what started as disappointment developed into devastation and depression. My plan had not been God's plan for me. Although I didn't understand at the time, He had directed my step (or misstep) that day to lead me down a path of faith that would ultimately save me from myself.

The good news is that I still attended the Division I college and I still ran track. The bad news is that I never fully recovered from the Achilles injury. My running career hit a frustrating plateau, leaving me hopeless, confused, and struggling emotionally. During college I battled mightily with bulimia due to the anxiety of coping with an injury. I felt as if I had never lived up to my own expectations or the expectations of my parents and coaches. I still trained with the track team and ran in some of the meets, but over time I lost all hope of a full recovery, and my contribution to the team felt pointless. I had put so much of my identity and purpose in life into running that life itself now began to feel meaningless. An emotional train wreck, I was spiraling down and could hide no longer.

Following two agonizing years of college, working out and living in the athletic trainer's clinic, I entered my track coach's office with plans to tell him about my eating disorder and let him know I was quitting the team. With tears flowing down my cheeks, I painstakingly shared my struggle with bulimia and depression and announced my decision to quit. I'll never forget the words of hope my coach, the man who'd recruited and believed in me, spoke to my hurting heart that day.

He graciously asked me to stay. Despite the fact I was not able to place or score points in a meet, coach asked me to stay on the team, because he said I was good for morale.

I nearly choked on my tears. My coach validated me as a person! He assessed value to me and my contribution to the team in a way I had not perceived, and he gave me a reason to move forward with life. He asked me to accept the role that God had for me and to take the next step in faith, wherever God wanted to lead me.

My college coach gave me a new hope and a purpose, some-thing I had slowly lost in the dark shadows of an injury and an eating disorder. I was good for morale. Ironically, the antonym to morale is aimlessness, a word that described my life at that mo-ment. He saw the truth at a time when I only believed the lies. Proverbs 16:24 says, "Gracious words are a honeycomb, sweet to the soul and healing to the bones." God knew I needed a kind but authoritative healing touch, so he used my coach to bring life, hope and healing to my fragile condition.

Psalm 40:3 says, "He put a new song in my mouth, a hymn of praise to our God. Many will see and fear the Lord and put their trust in him." We see this concept of new song modeled in Scripture by the likes of David, Hannah, Zechariah, and Mary, to name a few. In fact, Ephesians 5:19–20 reminds us that when we are filled with the Spirit we should "speak to one another with psalms, hymns, and songs from the Spirit," and, "sing and make music from your heart to the Lord, always giving thanks to God the Father for everything, in the name of our Lord Jesus Christ." My coach helped place a new hope and a new song in my heart, which is exactly where we find Mary, on the coattails of Elizabeth's praise and thanksgiving in the presence of her Lord.

After Elizabeth's life-giving words of hope and her affirmation of Mary's calling, Mary responded as a woman set free to love the Lord with all her heart, soul, mind, and strength. What follows Mary's encounter with Elizabeth in Luke chapter 1 is referred to as the Magnificat. The Latin *Magnificat* means "proclaims the great-ness." By the work of the Spirit, Elizabeth helped transform Mary's thinking and fragile emotional condition into a song of thanksgiv-ing and praise for who God is, proclaiming His greatness in her life as well as all of Israel.

God gave Mary a new song, founded in truth, offered in love, and inspired by the Holy Spirit. Leaving behind all doubts and fears about a possible life of rejection, Mary was filled with a new hope of a Savior, and she could rejoice in the work of God's hands. Her sacrifice of praise, Mary's song, is found in Luke 1:46–55:

> And Mary said: "My soul glorifies the Lord and my spirit rejoices in God my Savior, for he has been mindful of the humble state of his servant. From now on all generations will call me blessed, for the Mighty One has done great things for me—holy is his name. His mercy extends to those who fear him, from generation to generation. He has performed mighty deeds with his arm; he has scattered those who are proud in their inmost thoughts. He has brought down rulers from their thrones but has lifted up the humble. He has filled the hungry with good things but has sent the rich away empty. He has helped his servant Israel, remembering to be merciful to Abraham and his descendants forever, just as he promised our ancestors."

In these moments of revelation and praise, Mary recognized that she was made in the image of God and that her very soul glorified and magnified the Lord. As an obedient servant, she was now an active reflection of Him. Mary's spirit had become one with the Holy Spirit, as she rejoiced in God for who He was, both Savior and Lord. Mary was humbled that God saw her as she was. He had given thought to her life in great detail and had placed great value on her role in His kingdom. Mary knew she would be called blessed for many generations to come, but not because of her own merit. The Mighty One had called her and empowered her to fulfill her holy calling as the mother of the long-awaited Messiah.

Mary continued to praise God in song for His mercy to those who fear him. She had tasted God's mercy in His calling on her life, and she discovered that it was good. God's plan may not have been what she expected or hoped; nevertheless, she began to view God's will for her life as a blessing, a fulfillment of prophecy, and a risk worth taking despite the costs. God's unique ability to turn the tide and create a paradox transferred Mary's fear of rejection and broken relationship with Joseph and her own family into a reverent fear of the only One who could love her unconditionally. As God shifted Mary's thinking from her worldly identity, hopes, and dreams to a more eternal perspective, she was free to proclaim the greatness of God and the mighty works of His hands.

Mary's recollection of all that God had done in Israel's history also served as a foretaste of all that he would do in the life and ministry of Jesus, her child. Phrases such as "scattered the proud," "brought down rulers," "lifted up the humble," "filled the hungry," and "sent the rich away" (Lk. 1:51–53) would eventually describe the work of the very One she carried in her womb. Little did Mary know the power of her spoken word as she praised God and sang a new song. She was a woman fully committed to God and His calling. Mary proclaimed the provision and promises of God to His people from generation to generation, referring to His covenant with Abraham, which would be fulfilled ultimately in Jesus.

Evidently spending time with Elizabeth helped Mary, but spending time under the influence of the Holy Spirit had changed her. Elizabeth's timely words of encouragement through the prompting of the Holy Spirit had infused an undeniable hope into Mary's heart, allowing her to fully embrace the love of God and His calling on her life. I envision Mary facing heaven with arms stretched wide, as if to embrace the full magnitude of God's mercy and grace. Through the work of the Holy Spirit, her hope was renewed, and Mary could contain herself no longer. God had put a new song in her mouth and a hymn of praise on her lips.

God-ordained music is one of the highest forms of praise and worship when inspired by and centered on Him. Throughout history—from Old Testament worship services, to traditional hymns wrought with spiritual truth, to today's contemporary praise and worship that often echo Scripture—musicians and singers have held a sacred role in leading God's people into the presence of God.

Christian music and song have the power to elevate God to His rightful place on the throne and encourage His people to rise above their circumstances and problems, so they can catch a glimpse of His Kingdom.

Music and song are also reciprocal when it comes to God. As we lift our praise and worship to Him through song, He pours His Spirit back into us, giving us a new perspective, a fresh look, and a new song. One evidence of Jesus setting a soul free is a woman who freely expresses her gratitude, praise ,and adoration of God Himself. At conversion, we not only become new creatures in Christ (2 Cor. 5:17), but God puts a new song in our hearts and minds that inevitably flows from our lips. As devoted Christ followers, we begin to live and breathe and have our being according to the rhythm and timing of our Maker.

During the darkest days of my depression, I felt indifferent and numb toward music and song. Music didn't move me like it had before, because my heart was hardened and my mind was filled with deceptive thoughts based on lies and painful memories. But Jesus says in John 8:32 (NIV), "Then you will know the truth, and the truth will set you free."

When my coach shared truth with me about my position and purpose on the track team, something in me changed. Although the change wasn't immediate, this interaction was a defining moment when truth began to filter into my thoughts, and my mind began to be set free from the lies. I began to live again in a way I had forgotten since my injury. Slowly but surely, with many bumps in the road, I sought after God, making Him a priority in my life. I began to sense a new song in my heart and to live more to the rhythm and timing of my Maker.

When is the last time you proclaimed the greatness of God? Spend some time pondering the important people and defining moments in your life and reflect on how God used them to bring you closer to Him. Also ponder some of the attributes of God, His character, and His promises. Can you remember a time in your life when God gave you a new hope and a new song? What was it? Would you be able to write it down in song form? Give it a try! Take some time to compose your own "Magnificat"!

PRAYER

Oh God, Your magnificence inspires my own Magnificat! My soul bursts at the thought of You and Your great love for me. My spirit longs to glorify Your name in all the earth. You alone are worthy of praise and thanksgiving for how far You have brought me, filtered through the hands of your mercy and grace. Thank You for the life-giving words of hope and promise spoken through the life of Your Son, Jesus Christ. May time spent with You give us a new hope and a new song, as we worship You in Spirit and in Truth and proclaim Your greatness for eternity. In Jesus's name. Amen!

Chapter Six

Joseph's Decision to Love Sacrificially

When Joseph woke up, he did what the angel of the
Lord had commanded him and took Mary home as
his wife.

—Matthew 1:24

Divorce is a dirty word in my house. As a child of divorce at age three, I didn't start grieving the loss of an intact family until I was a teenager, a process that took years of sorting through painful questions and an acceptance of hard realities. By the grace of God, I eventually discovered the freedom that comes through forgiveness when I forgave my parents. If there was one thing I knew beyond a shadow of a doubt going into my own marriage, it was that I *never* wanted to get divorced. It was that simple: divorce was not an option, until the day I found myself standing in a similar position as my mother had, when she came face to face with the decision to stay or to leave.

The first several years of my marriage were less than pleasant, to put it mildly. The honeymoon phase did not survive long under the heavy demands of a new business and a new baby. While I worked full-time and took care of a newborn, my husband worked tirelessly to start a company to provide for his family, just as he had seen his father do. Unfortunately, over time *not* spent communicating or enjoying each other, our marriage relationship grew distant and our hearts resentful as our home grew cold and uninviting. I was an amateur wife with post-partum blues. I felt abandoned in my own home, with a baby who needed more than I had to give emotionally. I was standing in my own mother's shoes because she had experienced a similar situation with my father.

There were days I thought God was playing a bad joke on me. I had a hard decision to make. I could stand firm in my conviction to never get a divorce, or I could give into the temptation to leave and make it on my own, because in my mind I was doing it all by myself anyway. I could feel my convictions crumbling under the stress, so in my desperation I reached out to a Christian counselor for help. It was a marriage-saving decision I will never regret.

God led me to a Christian counselor through the recommendation of a friend. Early on, my husband told me I was the one who needed counseling, so I went alone. However, over time I convinced him to join me, and the counselor helped us reach the heart of the matter. We began a long journey learning about the realities of love—not as the world defines it, but sacrificial love as Jesus demonstrates it.

Our counselor, who is now our pastor, told us a story about the advice his mentor had given him many years prior when he was struggling in his own marriage. The mentor turned to him and boldly, yet lovingly in true Jesus fashion, told him that he needed to go home and love his wife.

"What?" The pastor was confused. "Go home and love my wife? What does that have to do with spreading the Kingdom of God?"

The mentor continued. "Go home and love your wife and children. What you do in the four walls of your home will do more for the Kingdom of God than any amount of preaching, teaching, or reaching."

During a time in our marriage when love felt like a distant memory and a small business and small children nearly consumed us, my husband and I heeded our counselor's advice and went home and loved each other sacrificially in the Spirit of Christ, without expecting anything in return.

Through the grace of God and the diligent work of the Holy Spirit, my husband and I began to experience the transforming power of God's love in our home. As the initial love that had first attracted us, bonded us, engaged us, and married us waned over time, God began teaching us about a love that never fails. The same love that held Jesus on the cross and calls us as children into the arms of Abba is a love tightly braided with faith and hope. It's the same love in 1 Corinthians 13:13, where "these three remain: faith, hope and love. But the greatest of these is love." It is a love that covers a multitude of sins. We began to let God love us so we could, in turn, love one another.

In Matthew 1:19–24, following the genealogy of Jesus, we find Joseph and Mary's relationship on rocky ground. Here we get a glimpse of Mary's story told from Joseph's perspective:

Because Joseph her husband was faithful to the law, and yet did not want to expose her to public disgrace, he had in mind to divorce her quietly. But after he had considered this, an angel of the Lord appeared to him in a dream and said, "Joseph son of David, do not be afraid to take Mary home as your wife, because what is conceived in her is from the Holy Spirit. She will give birth to a son, and you are to give him the name Jesus, because he will save his people from their sins." . . . When Joseph woke up, he did what the angel of the Lord had commanded him and took Mary home as his wife.

Within these verses we find Joseph alone and confused, perhaps fuming over the news of Mary's alleged infidelity. Perhaps he was angry, perhaps he was hurt that she didn't come tell him herself, or perhaps he was embarrassed to the extent of feeling emasculated. Matthew spares us the details of Joseph's broken heart; however, he exposes enough of his emotional reaction to reveal Joseph's intention to divorce Mary quietly as a result of this devastating news. Although they had not yet consummated the marriage, Matthew refers to Joseph as Mary's husband and calls him "faithful to the law," meaning he was a righteous man, one of integrity and moral fortitude. Betrothal was dissolvable only by divorce. As a righteous man, Joseph had every right to divorce Mary, based on her alleged violation of their marriage covenant.

God knew Joseph would respond to the shocking news by secretly planning to divorce Mary quietly. By law, Mary could have been put to death. Not wanting to publicly disgrace her, Joseph's thoughts alone reflected the depth of his love for Mary, despite the disgrace she had heaped upon him. His love for Mary would serve to protect her, but her alleged dishonor could have driven away the man she loved. Joseph's love could not overcome his fear of being disrespected. God knew Joseph's wound of betrayal by his betrothed would end all hope of a happily ever after, so he sent an angel who echoed the words spoken to Mary: "Do not be afraid."

The angel Gabriel, the same messenger God sent to Mary, tells Joseph that, in essence, "Joseph, it's okay. Go home and love your wife. Go home and love your Son, Jesus. He is a gift of the Holy Spirit. He is the One who saves." And that is exactly what Joseph did. He reunited with Mary after she returned from visiting Elizabeth. In God's perfect timing, He exchanged confusion for clarity and doubt for hope. He restored love where shame threatened to keep two hearts from becoming one. Joseph trusted God with the truth about his bride, thereby giving up his good reputation and bringing reproach on his family. Joseph obediently went home and sacrificially loved Mary as one who was called, chosen, and ordained by God.

One of the worst things a woman can do to a man is disrespect him. Trust me, I know. During the early years of my marriage I did not offer my husband the respect he desired because of my own unmet expectations and resentful heart. Ephesians 5:22–24 gives specific instructions to wives to submit, which means to honor and respect her husband:

> Wives, submit yourselves to your own husbands as you do to the Lord. For the husband is the head of the wife as Christ is the head of the church, his body, of which he is the Savior. Now as the church submits to Christ, so also wives should submit to their husbands in everything.

Wives are commanded to honor, respect, and submit to their husbands, because God knows in His infinite wisdom that loving and nurturing come more naturally to a woman, while honoring and respecting usually don't. Women need the command to respect, because it is the lifeline for a man to feel respected and give love in return. On the flip side, if you read further in Ephesians 5, husbands are commanded to love their wives. While honor and respect are the primal language of man, loving and nurturing take more intentional effort for a husband. Men need the command to love, because it is the lifeline for a woman to feel loved and give respect in return. In God's infinite wisdom, He knows our nature and instructs us likewise.

Divorce, even in cases where it is warranted and justified (such as abuse), is hard and ugly and painful. It houses a lifetime of repercussions for every generation that follows the severed relationship of a husband and wife, especially when they are called Dad and Mom. Despite being a product of divorce and having lived through the repercussions, there was a time in my marriage when I was at the cliff of marital discord, prepared to jump, parachute or not. I was so deceived that I was willing to choose and experience the pain of tearing a family apart over the pain of not getting my needs met. Pain is selfish and, when left to its own way, will lead you down the road to destruction.

God in His mercy talked me away from that dreadful cliff and helped me dig in my heels and plant my white flag of surrender to Him and His way for my marriage and family. It took years of waiting, hoping, praying, leaving and cleaving, and counseling. Along the way I allowed God to become my Sustainer, my Hope, my Source of authentic Love, and the One for whom I walked in faith. During the days in my marriage when only faith remained, I chose God and trusted Him to teach me to respect and love my husband sacrificially.

Joseph is a wonderful example of someone obedient to the call to love sacrificially, and there is another jewel concerning sacrificial love to uncover in Joseph's decision to take Mary as his wife. The day Joseph woke from his Gabriel dream, slumbering on God's direction for his life, and said yes to his calling to love, honor, and cherish Mary, he also said yes to Jesus for the very first time. By going home and loving Mary, Joseph also committed to going home and loving his son Jesus as His adoptive father, despite the gossip. Joseph chose to sacrificially love Mary and Jesus despite the cost.

Jesus was conceived by the Holy Spirit. Therefore Joseph adopted Jesus into his own family, only later to discover that

Jesus would make the way for each of us to be adopted into the family of God. Many adoptive parents have told me it isn't just the child who is saved, but it is often the parents who receive the blessing of saving grace from the child. A friend adopted after several years of trying to get pregnant. She told me it suddenly all made sense, the moment she held her baby boy for the first time, why she had to endure the pain and loss of infertility and multiple miscarriages. The giving and receiving of new life into her outstretched arms helped heal and restore her heart, so she could love the child sacrificially as her own, despite the pain she had endured.

At the heart of adoption is a sacrificial love that extends beyond skin color and blood type, national borders and ethnic traditions, chromosomal abnormalities and fear of the unknown. Joseph said yes to Jesus and loved Him as his own child, only to receive the blessing of saving grace. Joseph did for Jesus what God had in mind for all creation through Jesus—to leave no one as an orphan (Matt. 14:18). In blessing Jesus with an earthly mother and father, God allowed Jesus to grow in favor and stature and provide a way for all to come to their heavenly Father at the cross.

Following the model of obedience of His own earthly parents, Jesus echoed their submission to God's will as He washed His disciple's feet and later traveled the grueling path toward Calvary. Christ was willing to demonstrate the sacrificial love of God from the cross so that no one will perish, but that all will have eternal life. This is why the ground is level at the foot of the cross. God's love is not limited by fear of what He may find out about you, because He already knows! He will not leave us as orphans. He will come to us, first by filling us with His Spirit, then again one day in Person.

If you are in Christ, you do not have an orphan spirit. You are not alone. The Holy Spirit dwells in you, sealed as a guarantee of Christ's return for your soul. He claims you, calls you, and compels you to draw closer and closer to Him, a Father to the fatherless. Crawl into His lap, like Jesus surely did with Joseph. Bounce on His knee and live freely in His presence, knowing you are loved and accepted as His child.

PRAYER

Heavenly Father, You love us with an unconditional, sacrificial love that surpasses all we could ask or imagine. Help us experience that love in a life-changing way through the power of Your Holy Spirit in our families, our friendships, our marriages, and with our children. Transform our selfish minds into selfless motives to love in the name of Jesus despite the cost because You, God, are our reward. In Jesus's name. Amen.

CHAPTER SEVEN

A Baby Changes Everything

He changes times and seasons.

—Daniel 2:21

My husband and I had only been married six months when I gave birth to our firstborn son. And no, he wasn't premature. I was the one prematurely pregnant the day we said, "I do." Although the wedding was planned, the pregnancy was not. This was because of my own foolish choices and, ultimately, God's sovereign intervention in my life. You may be asking yourself, *what kind of Jesus-loving girl does this?* Honestly, I had to ask myself the same question, and with full transparency I can tell you what kind of girl gets pregnant two or three months before her wedding day. A girl who is too insecure and broken to say, "Let's wait," and a girl who naively thought the chances of pregnancy were slim. It sounds pathetic, but insecurities have a way of lying to us. Wisdom comes only with age, experience, and time spent learning the hard lessons of life.

At one point before I walked down the church aisle to pledge my love and my life, my guilty conscience wandered into the story of *The Scarlet Letter*. Instead of a big "A" for adultery, I thought I deserved a big "I" for idiot, or for idol, for making everything about me and my own desires. My life seemed as if I had done everything backward:

- moved in with my boyfriend
- started a business together
- got engaged
- got pregnant
- got married
- got on my knees, broken and afraid.

However, during a time in my life when I had no idea what I was doing, God in His infinite wisdom knew exactly what He was doing.

From the moment I saw the plus sign on the pregnancy stick, I can testify that a baby changes everything. I was twenty-eight and still in the throes of a fifteen-year battle with bulimia. Although I was managing the addictive behavior somewhat better through counseling, the shock and anxiety of getting pregnant, compounded with the stress of planning a wedding, sent me into a tailspin of emotional turmoil with a high probability of a crash and burn. The weight of guilt and shame from my secret addiction and a secret pregnancy became intolerable burdens that forced me to my knees. I was broken before a heavenly Father who was waiting with open arms. I was the prodigal who had no choice but to go home and stare into the failure and disappointment on my own father's face. It was time to be completely honest with myself, with my family, and most importantly with God.

And so, over the next eight to nine months, God brought me to my knees in the wake of an infant business, an infant marriage, and an infant developing in my womb. I remember sitting alone on my bed one night in tears, desperately crying out to God in a way I never had before. Over the course of the first and second trimesters, as my baby bump appeared and I started acknowledging my own self-centeredness and that invisible "I" on my chest, I began to come to terms with my life, my condition, my foolish choices, my failures, and ultimately my sins.

Praying to God, I confessed, "God, You know I'm saved. You know I gave my life to Christ at an early age. But God, I need You to save me from myself right now, because it's not about me anymore." As the baby within filled my womb and grew closer to my heart, life became less about me and my desires and expectations, and more about God and His will for my life through the new life of my child.

Alone with God in my bedroom, I rededicated my life to Christ that night and asked Him to heal me from the inside out. All the counseling and years of trying to be better and do better on my own had only focused on fixing and healing me from the outside in. Only Jesus can transform and heal our brokenness from the inside out. I asked God for what seemed like a miracle—that He would take the taste of bulimia from my lips, just as I had witnessed Him take the taste of alcohol from the lips of an alcoholic family member. I was ready to fully surrender to Jesus, not just as my Savior, but also as the Lord of my life. During those precious months of development and growth, I began a journey. Like the child within me, I grew from an infant faith to trusting a Father God who raises His daughters and sons into the likeness of His own Son.

I remember the first time I heard the song "A Baby Changes Everything," by Faith Hill, during an Advent service at church. I sat in tears of awe as I listened to Mary's experience played out in song—a young girl unprepared for a baby who changes everything. If you aren't familiar with the song and you want to cry like a baby, go ahead and Google it. This song sets the stage beautifully for Mary's birth story, where the ideal couple, with their hope and love in one another restored, experience the not-so-ideal birth of Hope and Love personified. Luke 2:1–7 tells the story, beginning with the arduous journey to Bethlehem:

> In those days Caesar Augustus issued a decree that a census should be taken of the entire Roman world . . . And everyone went to their own town to register. So Joseph also went up from the town of Nazareth in Galilee to Judea, to Bethlehem the town of David, because he belonged to the house and line of David. He went there to register with Mary, who was pledged to be married to him and was expecting a child. While they were there, the time came for the baby to be born, and she gave birth to her firstborn, a son. She wrapped him in cloths and placed him in a manger, because there was no guest room available for them.

The nurses at the hospital told me you could have taken a census in the waiting room before my firstborn finally decided to make his appearance. After almost twenty-two hours of labor, an epidural, and a short nap, we added one to our family of two and a huge celebration erupted down the hall. The not-so-ideally-timed pregnancy had given birth to the not-so-ideal labor (thirty-six hours of no sleep combined with twenty-two hours of labor equals a horrible start to parenting). Thus was born the baby who changed everything for my husband and me. There was no more time to ponder a guilty conscience, and the invisible "I" was about to be covered with spit up anyway. We took our little one home and swaddled him in love and thanksgiving for the grace, mercy, and forgiveness God bestows on rookie parents.

Similarly, Joseph and Mary began their journey in parenting with an unplanned pregnancy, an unplanned journey to Bethlehem, and a not-so-ideal labor and delivery. God's timing and His working of His will, even in the lives of nonbelievers, never ceases to amaze me. In this case, God used the Roman Emperor Caesar

Augustus (a name meaning *exalted*) to call an empire-wide census for the purpose of taxation and military service to draw Joseph back to his roots with his betrothed. Ponder that for a moment. God used power, money, and pride to work out a prophecy that Jesus would be born in Bethlehem, and hardly anyone noticed.

Joseph and Mary's journey from Nazareth, where they first fell in love, to Bethlehem, where they would give birth to Love Himself, was significant. Scholars predict the ninety-mile journey would have taken three days. And I was worried about my five-minute drive to the hospital! Mary, I hope, got to ride on a donkey those long, three days from Nazareth, traveling south through Jerusalem to Bethlehem. Do you see any parallels to Jesus's journey to the cross? A donkey, three days, Jerusalem . . . God's divine use of foreshadowing and repetition in Scripture is one of the ways He gets our attention. And if we are paying attention, God does what I call "connecting the dots."

Do you think Mary knew that her labor-intensive trip to Bethlehem foreshadowed her own Son's labor-intensive journey to the cross? At that point on her journey of faith how could she know? Mary was simply obedient to God and to her beloved Joseph. Mary's obedience had taken her from an encounter with an angel to the birthplace of a Savior and the fulfillment of ancient prophecy. We seldom know the ripple effect of our simple obedience, especially when we cannot see the end result.

I imagine this ninety-mile hike from Nazareth to Bethlehem was somewhat labor inducing, but maybe that's because my water broke with my firstborn after just a few hours of Christmas shopping. Nevertheless, Scripture says when they were in Bethlehem, the time had come. Can you imagine what was going through Mary's heart and mind, much less her abdomen, as she and Joseph looked for a place to rest and prepare? Perhaps Mary was perplexed that such an important calling to give birth to the Son of the Most High could lead her to such an unfamiliar, far away, lonely and lowly place. She was three days away from home. Three days away from her mother, sisters, friends, and Elizabeth, and oh, how she must have longed for Elizabeth's presence. But she had arrived at this vital moment with Joseph, and perhaps this was the first of many "leave and cleave" lessons for Mary. God had provided Joseph, her betrothed, and now came God's provision of a stable—a humble yet well-protected place for Mary to rest and prepare.

The timing didn't seem ideal, the place less than hoped for, and the outcome uncertain, but imagine, in these moments of exhaustion and thanksgiving between contractions, Mary leaning into God harder than ever before in total dependence. This may not have been the way Mary dreamed of starting a marriage and a family, but this was the way God had designed and set into motion. It was His plan of salvation for the world and His forever family. God was working out an eternal plan in Mary's journey.

I can relate to Mary's experience, because I had never dreamed of getting pregnant before I was married. I never wanted to struggle with so much responsibility and uncertainty in the first several years of my marriage. As a young girl, I dreamed of being swept off my feet by the perfect man for a lifetime of happily ever after. Yet God taught me that through the consequences of my poor choices and the times I lived outside His will, God causes everything to work together for the good of those who love Him and are called according to His purpose (Rom. 8:28). God just wants us, like Mary, to lean into Him in total dependence, regardless of where life takes us.

God uses everything, even when everything doesn't make sense to us. No doubt Mary's world did not make a lot of sense in the waves of labor pains, with Joseph as her midwife and perhaps a few of Noah's Ark creatures looking on. Nevertheless, she swaddled and nursed her baby as motherly instincts awoke from deep within. She laid the Bread of Life in a feeding trough because the world had not made room for him. At least not yet. Mary's birth story continues in Luke 2:8–20:

And there were shepherds living out in the fields nearby, keeping watch over their flocks at night. An angel of the Lord appeared to them, and the glory of the Lord shone around them, and they were terrified. But the angel said to them, "Do not be afraid. I bring you good news that will cause great joy for all the people. Today in the town of David a Savior has been born to you; he is the Messiah, the Lord." . . . So they hurried off and found Mary and Joseph, and the baby, who was lying in the manger. When they had seen him, they spread the word concerning what had been told them about this child . . . But Mary treasured up all these things and pondered them in her heart.

This has to be the birth announcement of all birth announcements! I've seen some pretty cute ones and some pretty corny ones, like the one with baby's picture inside an old-fashioned clock with the caption, "Meet Our New Alarm Clock." However, the divine birth announcement song to the shepherds by a host of angels tops them all. And if you listen closely, you will hear the echo of Gabriel telling Mary as well as Joseph just nine months before: "Do not be afraid. I bring you good news" (Lk. 2:10). God used the greatest birth announcement of all time to tell some of the lowliest and humblest of men—shepherds working the night shift—of the birth of the long-awaited Messiah. Only God could send the heavenliest creatures to the earthliest men and make sense in the backdrop of a divine birth in a barn!

Scholars say that these men were shepherds for the temple lambs who, without spot or blemish, would find their destiny on the altar of sacrifice and atonement. And once again, only God would plan to tell the shepherds of unblemished lambs that the Perfect One was born. This perfect Lamb would one day find His destiny on the cross of sacrifice and atonement, once and for all. Little did these shepherds know the significance of this announcement. Not only would lambs one day be freed from a destiny of slaughter, but mankind would soon be freed from spiritual death, Hell, and the grave. Jesus is the good news that will bring great joy for all people!

This is also the first time the gospel, which means good news, was preached. This event caused the gates of heaven to swing wide open and a host of angels to appear from the throne room of God, singing, "Glory to God in the highest heaven, and on earth peace to those on whom his favor rests" (Lk. 2:14). The shepherds caught a glimpse of heaven and of God's glory that night, and they hurried off to find Mary and Joseph and a baby lying in a manger. There is nothing like an encounter with God to stir the fire of the Holy Spirit within you and ignite your passion here on earth. God handpicked these shepherds to spread the gospel of peace that the long-awaited, much-anticipated Messiah was here in the town of David.

I wonder if Mary and Joseph could hear the shepherds out on a treasure hunt through Bethlehem to find the babe swaddled in a manger? I wonder how many stables or caves they went to before they found the one with newborn life? Imagine the look on Mary's face when she realized that her baby's first visitors were not blood relatives but rugged, smelly shepherds. Perhaps God used this not-so-ideal and somewhat intrusive visit and transcended it into the spiritual realm for Mary and Joseph's listening hearts to comprehend the magnitude of this night in Bethlehem. Time must have stopped in those moments for Mary, as she "treasured up all these things and pondered them in her heart" (Lk. 2:19). Maybe the shock of labor and the shakes of adrenaline had subsided, but there must have been a quaking in her heart that night as she heard the shepherds herald the message of her Son's birth. This secret wasn't just for Joseph and her anymore. This was for the whole world to know. Jesus the Messiah is born! Emmanuel, God with us!

As the dust settled in the stable and Mary pondered herself to sleep, the shepherds returned to their flocks, glorifying and praising

God for showing Himself faithful. They had found everything just as they had been told. No doubt about it, these were changed men. They had started their night with hopes for an uneventful sheep watch, but their night ended having seen the glory of God, a host of His angels, His Son in the flesh, and—to top it off—they had been filled with the Spirit as they worshiped the Author of it all. God had sent shepherds to confirm the birth of the Good Shepherd to Mary, to Joseph, and to all of us who are like sheep and gone astray.

Will you hang out in Luke chapter 2 for a while with Mary and ponder the baby who changes everything? Who or what has God used in your life to change the way you see God or view yourself? What do you still need to surrender to God in order to draw closer and lean in with total dependence? Mary was chosen by God to be the mother of the Messiah, not because of who she was, but because of who God is. God has also chosen you to play a part in His Kingdom. Before you start squirming like Moses, thinking you are unworthy and unqualified, let me remind you that God can handle all your baggage. He can handle your mistakes, your failures, your insecurities, your shame, your past, and even your dumb ideas! God turned my mess into my message, and He will do the same for you. He will use *anything* in order to become your *everything*.

PRAYER

Dear God, You desire us to rededicate our lives to You each and every day. Help us surrender to the truth that you work all things together for good for those who love You, even the things we try to hide. Like Mary, help us through faith to trust in Your plan for our lives, even when it doesn't make sense. In Jesus's name. Amen.

CHAPTER EIGHT

Mary Had a Little Lamb

*And he came in the Spirit into the temple, and when
the parents brought in the child Jesus, to do for him
according to the custom of the Law, he took him up
in his arms and blessed God and said . . .*

—*Luke 2:27–28* ESV

For anyone who has ever parented a child, you have undoubtedly experienced the moment when the bubble of parenting bliss, joy, sunshine, and giggles is unexpectedly and shockingly burst by reality. Maybe it happened to you during your first sleepless night, like day two of baby's life. Don't feel bad. There is a certain blessing in getting the "we have the perfect child" syndrome over and done with. Or maybe it happened much later, when your baby was twelve months old and looked into your loving mommy eyes and said, "No!" for the first time. My personal favorite was when green pea baby food found its way onto the ceiling as a result of a mealtime temper tantrum. Oh no! The bubble popped, with the messy realities of parenting staring me right in the face.

Parenting realities come in all shapes and sizes. Some are anticipated, but the majority arrive quite unexpectedly. Like the day my firstborn, age three, and my second child, age nine months, got into their first fight. Are you kidding me? Siblings fight at this age? I called my husband (the oldest of four), crying, "They hate each other. What have I done?" only to hear hysterical laughter coming from the other end. My husband, in all his sibling wisdom, said, "Siblings fight. Get used to it." Parenting Reality 101.

That had not been my reality growing up. My childhood was a world of one for the first seven years. My parents were divorced, and my stepsisters didn't live with us, so when my half-brother was born I was primed and ready for a real-life baby doll. Having no competition and no reason to fight, I welcomed my baby brother with open arms. But that was not the case for my children. As soon as the nine-month-old could pull up to eye level with the three-year-old's world, the fight was on! All those days prior, sitting outside blowing bubbles to children in the wind? The bubbles kept bursting.

I was blessed to spend twelve short, sweet, sleepless weeks at home with my firstborn son. Sweet memories flood my mind of reclining on the couch in my pajamas, the sour smell of spit up in my hair, as I gazed at my precious newborn resting between my legs. I was awestruck at the miracle of a tiny life, my helpless babe. God had formed him in my womb and birthed him from my frame. God had entrusted this baby miracle to me, and he was mine for a time to love, nurture, and care for.

Then there was the day the needle of parenting reality felt like it penetrated my soul after bursting through the bubble of maternity leave. Unfortunately, the days of staring at my son as he slept peacefully in my arms, with no place to go and no place to be, came to an inevitable end. This new mama had to go back to work. My short reality of maternity leave was over, and my new reality of being a working mom was about to begin. I have one word for this experience: heartwrenching. And if you've been there, you know.

The morning came when I had to pack up my baby bundle along with the diaper bag, extra breast milk, car seat—the entire kitchen sink—and drive to my mother-in-law's house. I left my baby and all his belongings there with Grandma. It was heartbreaking, and this was an ideal situation! Family was becoming the extension of my loving, nurturing motherly arms and yet, it felt as if my heart was torn in two that first morning I drove to work empty-handed. I know, it's a bit dramatic, but when it's your baby and your reality, it's your drama and your pain. Reality hits hard when idealism and realism collide, and you have to entrust your firstborn son into the care of another.

Likewise it was for Mary and Joseph the day they took their newborn Son to the temple in Jerusalem, an account found in Luke 2:21–38. Luke tells us that Jesus was circumcised on the eighth day according to Jewish tradition. Following circumcision, the days of purification lasted another thirty-three days, according to the law in Leviticus 12:1–8. Therefore, when Joseph and Mary entered the temple in Jerusalem it had been a total of forty days since Jesus had taken His first breath, forty days since the shepherds had shared the good news, and forty days for Mary to ponder in her heart the significance of her Son's birth in a manger. After forty days, a number laden with significance and foreshadowing, Mary obediently went to the temple for personal purification and presented her little Lamb on the altar of praise, thanksgiving, and dedication to the Lord (Luke 2:21–38).

As God had ordained, the Law of Moses required the mother of a newborn child to bring the priest a year-old lamb for a burnt offering and a pigeon or a turtledove for a sin offering, for the purpose of making atonement for her and making her clean. However, if the mother could not afford a lamb, then she should take two turtledoves or two pigeons, one for a burnt offering and the other for a sin offering. Luke implies that Mary and Joseph only brought turtledoves or pigeons to the temple that day. Yet out of their own poverty they presented heaven's greatest treasure. They brought the Lamb of God before the priest to be dedicated.

As obedient Jewish parents, they arrived at the temple, no doubt unified in mind, heart, and spirit with the desire for their firstborn Son to know the Lord their God, the Mighty One of Israel, and to be dedicated unto His service. Mary and Joseph wanted Jesus, their little Lamb, to follow in their footsteps of faith, to love the Lord their God and grow in His favor and His blessing.

Like most parents, Mary and Joseph realized that their child was entrusted to them only for a time. Children are a gift from God, and family is God's most powerful tool in expanding His Kingdom. Therefore, His parents brought Jesus to the temple in the holy city of Jerusalem and presented Him back to His Father, the Holy God of Israel. When we as parents, grandparents, godparents, guardians, and fellow members of the body of Christ dedicate a life, we follow in the footsteps of the faith of Mary and Joseph.

This passage in Luke chapter 2 marks Jesus's first public debut, as well as Mary and Joseph's first public confession of faith in Jesus as God's child. What happened next, Mary never could have seen coming. The Holy Spirit had assured Simeon the prophet that he would live long enough to see the Messiah and prophesy in His name (vv. 29–32). Israel's "consolation" refers to the comfort and hope the people found in God's plan for His people and specifically the Messiah's role. After laying eyes on the newborn Jesus, Simeon took the baby from Mary and praised God as he prophesied in Jesus's name with references like "your salvation," "a light for revelation to the Gentiles," "glory to Your people Israel." Simeon announced to all in attendance the worldwide scope of the gospel—that salvation is for both Jew and Gentile. Then Simeon leaned into Mary to deliver a disturbing addendum.

On the day of your baby's dedication or christening, could you imagine your pastor or an elder of your church taking your baby right out of your hands and, after announcing God's great plans for the child, leaning in and whispering to you, "Behold, this child is appointed for the fall and rising of many in [your hometown], and for a sign that is opposed so that thoughts from many hearts may be revealed"? I'm sure I would choke and feel a dagger to my heart. What could all this possibly mean?

But Mary simply pondered. She listened and she pondered. In fact, she had been pondering for forty days, and now the inspired words of the Holy Spirit through the prophet Simeon, confirmed later by the prophetess Anna, had multiplied her reasons to continue pondering. In those inspired moments, the God of the universe, the Father of Jesus Himself, shined a light into the unknown darkness of the future to show a mother a glimpse of her Son's destiny. Providence, prophecy, destiny, and truth collided in those moments between Mary and a prophet and prophetess.

In his book *The Pressure's Off*, Dr. Larry Crab describes those desiring to live the "New Way": "They come as they are. They do not bathe before they approach God. They come to God for the bath." Mary had come to the priest that day for her ceremonial bath—to be cleansed from her own blood, purified, and granted atonement through the sacrifice presented by the priest. Yet Simeon's words of prophecy foretold the One who would soon cleanse us all by His own blood and purify our hearts from sin. Jesus would serve as the final atonement of sin through the sacrifice of Himself on the cross, and later ascend as our High Priest to sit at the right hand of God Almighty.

During the days of purification according to the Law of Moses, Mary was not to touch anything holy. But after her cleansing and atonement, and a baby dedication like no other, Mary would carry the Holy of Holies into His toddler years as He grew in stature and favor with God. Mary had a little Lamb that would one day take away the sins of the world. And Mary loved Him so.

The famous nursery rhyme "Mary Had a Little Lamb" is based on a true story about a girl named Mary who look her pet lamb to school one day. The rhyme was written by American school teacher Sarah Josephina Hale, who published the rhyme in May 1830.

Some sources think it is possible that John Roulstone, a seminary student at the time, wrote part of the poem and may have added a spiritual or moral dimension to the now-famous nursery rhyme. While most people are familiar with the first few lines, I encourage you to look up and read the poem in full. "Mary Had a Little Lamb" is one of the more palatable nursery rhymes of our day, and if we listen closely we can hear Jesus and His mother in this little ditty.

The lamb, like Jesus, was pure as snow. The lamb, like Jesus, first loved Mary and followed her everywhere she went. The lamb, like Jesus, broke the rules of the Pharisaical world and caused quite the ruckus wherever he went. The lamb, like Jesus, was turned out and rejected, but waited patiently for his hour to come. And the lamb, like Jesus, loved Mary first and longed for her presence.

"We love because He first loved us" (1 Jn. 4:19). Jesus's mother Mary had brought a little Lamb to the temple that day, but His hour had not yet come. According to the prophet Simeon, Mary's Lamb was the salvation God had promised. His coming would bring the rise and fall of many so that the hearts of man would be revealed. Jesus, the perfect Lamb slain on a cross-shaped altar of God's redemption, would be opposed and rejected. Mary held her little Lamb close as her "maternity leave" (literally six weeks, or forty-two days) was ending and a deeper work of faith was about to begin.

As a parent I can't imagine the thoughts going through Mary's mind as she left the temple that day. She must have replayed Simeon's words over and over. What did he mean by the "fall and rising of many" and a "sign that is opposed"? Perhaps she was afraid to even consider what Simeon meant by a "sword will pierce through your own soul." She may have also questioned God's will and plan for her Son. What bold, heartbreaking revelations about both Jesus and her own destiny as a mother! Mary had to choose to live in fear, with the anxiety of how this revelation would come to pass, or in faith, trusting God. When Simeon pulled the rug of hope out from under her, perhaps God's love felt ambiguous, but when only faith remained, Mary persevered in that faith. And like the newborn in her arms, Mary's faith was just beginning to grow as she pondered her encounters with God's messengers. Through Simeon and Anna, God shined a lamp unto her feet and light onto her path, but faith would propel her forward into a soul-piercing destiny as the mother of the Lamb of God.

Parenting requires faith, often in the absence of hope and reciprocated love, especially during the teenage years. Can I get a witness? As the mother of three children, I have experienced the tug-of-war between having a measure of control over my children and their daily lives and living by a maternal faith in God, who has the ultimate control over their destinies. Parenting is not for wimps. If we aren't mindful, the worry and anxiety that builds as our children grow and become more independent from our care and control can overwhelm us.

I never realized the way worry and anxiety had negatively affected me until I had children. While my eating disorder was a manifestation of a certain level of childhood anxiety, it wasn't until I had children that I realized how much anxiety and the need for control were controlling my life. After freeing me from the bondage of bulimia, God began peeling back the layers of my anxious heart and mind through the challenges of raising children. Over time, through the ups and downs of parenting, He graciously revealed to me the source of much of my worry and anxiety. God began a deeper work of faith in me by asking, "Do you believe I am who I say I am? Do you trust Me?" At the time, I thought I truly believed and trusted God, but I discovered you can only trust what you know to be true.

How well do you know God? How much time have you spent getting to know Him better? Do you believe He is who Scripture says He is? Have you spent time in His Word to discover His truth and His promises? Do you trust Him with every area of your life? These are all questions I had to answer myself as God revealed more of my anxious thoughts and habits. As a believer I desired to surrender more of my life to God, and as a parent I had the responsibility of raising my children in the Christian faith. God graciously invited me to walk a deeper path of faith in order to know Him and trust Him more. Eugene Peterson's *A Long Obedience in the Same Direction* is a description of our faith walk. When we set out on the path of faith in God, each step of obedience becomes a step closer to knowing God.

PRAYER

Father God, we confess that we can only trust You to the extent that we know and believe in You. Thank You for the gift of faith that allows us to take the long walk of obedience toward You and Your will. Reveal Yourself to us, Lord, so that we may know You and trust You more. In Jesus's name. Amen.

Chapter Nine

Finding the Light of the World

And going into the house, they saw the child with Mary his mother, and they fell down and worshiped him.

—*Matthew 2:11* ESV

When I was still a new mom juggling the demands of a toddler and a newborn, an observant friend kindly invited me to join a playgroup including other moms with children around the same age. I was a stay-at-home mom with limited adult interaction, so the invitation was in God's perfect timing to get me out of the house and into conversations and interactions with other moms who were experiencing similar circumstances and challenges. Playgroup was a fun time for the children to interact and learn to share. With insecurities as a new wife and mother dominating my thought life, playgroup became a source of knowledge, hope, and much-needed laughter for me. In His infinite wisdom, God directed my path to this caring and supportive group of women, although His plan didn't stop there.

Several weeks after I joined the playgroup, one of the women invited me to a Bible study that fit my schedule and included a children's program. This simple invitation would change my life forever. God had brought me to a playgroup for my children for the purpose of leading me into ministry and a life-changing study of Him through His Holy Word.

With a toddler and newborn in tow I joined Community Bible Study (CBS) and commenced a lifelong love and study of the Bible. Over the next several years, all three of my children attended CBS as preschoolers, before starting public school. This formed a foundation of biblical knowledge and truth they could build on through childhood and into their teens. God didn't waste any time calling me into a leadership role as a preschool teacher and later as a core leader, associate teaching director, and children and youth director. In awe I reflect back on how God called me into leadership, teaching preschoolers, for the purpose and divine timing of teaching me how to better parent my own children through His love, mercy, and grace.

God knew exactly when and where to lead me into a closer walk with Him. Bible study became a refuge. Through CBS, He helped me dive into the Word in a way I was struggling to do on my own. He also provided me with an expanded community of believers, beyond my own church family, to explore the promises of God. Through the vision of CBS, I've been transformed through the faithful study and application of His Word. Through the mission and ministry of CBS, I've become a disciple of the Word, the One who became flesh, Jesus Christ. What started with a friendly invitation led me to the Word Himself, a lamp unto my feet and the light unto my path (Ps. 119:105).

God knows exactly when, where, who, and what to use to ultimately lead us to Him. He's been working in the lives of humanity through signs and wonders, natural events, natural consequences, and natural curiosity for thousands of years. We see God do the same in the story of the wise men as He uses the orders from a pagan king and a bright star to lead them to the Light of the World.

Matthew 2:1–12 tells the story of the visit of the wise men, who came to Jerusalem from the East asking, "Where is he who has been born king of the Jews? For we saw his star when it rose and have come to worship him." This information troubled Herod and, after inquiring about the location of the birth from the chief priests and scribes, he secretly summoned the wise men and sent them to search for the child in Bethlehem.

A few years ago, a sweet family member noticed that my Willow Tree nativity set did not include the wise men. Weeks later a surprise package arrived on my doorstep. They had sent me the three wise men to complete my nativity collection. Adding the new wooden figurines to the display, I started thinking about these mysterious men. Although almost every nativity scene during Christmas includes the wise men, the wise men did not actually arrive until months or possibly years after Jesus's birth. What else do we not know or perhaps have forgotten about these men? Were there only three? How did the visit of the wise men affect Mary and Joseph? And what can God, through these mysterious visitors, reveal to us about our own journey of faith?

The visit of the Magi, or wise men, is only recorded in the Gospel of Matthew. No other gospel account includes their visit in the postpartum story. My study Bible (HCSB) explains that the summons of the Magi to visit Jesus demonstrates God's intention to save Gentiles from their futile religions. One reason why only Matthew included them in his gospel is his emphasis on including Gentiles in God's redemption story.

As the Scripture says, these Magi came from the East, most likely from Babylon or Persia. Interestingly, the word *Magi* for wise men in the Book of Matthew is also found in the book of Daniel. These Eastern Magi in Matthew, similar to the ones described in Daniel, are historically associated with mediums and sorcerers. They mixed Zoroastrianism (an ancient Persian religion) with astrology and black magic, and subsequently had a fascination with stars, comets and meteors. Why else would they travel so far to Jerusalem and then to Bethlehem? God can use anything to lead us to Him! As far back as Genesis chapter 41, we find Pharaoh also dabbled with wise men when he called on them to interpret his dreams. Then, when the wise men of Egypt were unable to do so, God's power enabled Joseph to interpret Pharaoh's dream.

What can we learn from these wise men who followed a star, only to find the Light of the World in a stable? Were they truly wise or just very curious? Were they genuinely seeking to worship Jesus or just the idea of Him? Let's look back at Matthew's description of the wise men's experience (Mt. 2:11–12 ESV):

> And going into the house, they saw the child with Mary his mother, and they fell down and worshiped him. Then, opening their treasures, they offered him gifts, gold and frankincense and myrrh. And being warned in a dream not to return to Herod, they departed to their own country by another way.

Perhaps when these men entered the house and met Jesus face to face, they were changed. As they stood face to face with the Word made flesh, their knees suddenly weak, their natural curiosity about a star was transformed into a supernatural desire to worship the Light of the World. Most likely God's grace trumped "wise"dom during this unexpected visit. God, in His preeminent wisdom, condescended to use pagan Magi superstitions about a star to draw them to Jesus, the Light of the World. Matthew says that after they worshiped Jesus, they responded to the Lord's leading, thereby thwarting Herod's plan, and went home a different way—literally taking a new direction in life. The visit of the Magi reminds us that Jesus transforms lives and God's grace covers both the wise man and the curious fool.

The wise men may not have been the only ones affected by this encounter with Jesus. Perhaps His parents were moved supernaturally when the Magi stopped by for a visit. It's unclear exactly when the wise men arrived, yet Scripture notes that Jesus was "by his mother's side." Young Jesus's world would have centered on Mary during his first several years, as she nursed and nurtured Him under the grace and favor of God. As the wise men entered the home to find Jesus with His mother, Mary must have recognized the look on their faces, a countenance she remembered on a few smelly shepherds at Jesus's birth. Joseph and Mary were most likely in awe at the response of worship their child evoked in this regal trio, with Joseph observing cautiously and Mary pondering.

God's mercy was evident in the visit of three wise men from the East with two young parents being prepared for the next step of faith. Herod's messengers may have brought gifts fit for a king; however, God used their covert mission to help warn two unsuspecting parents of the presence of trickery and evil. Even the gifts of gold, frankincense, and myrrh foreshadow the fate of a divine infant king. (Gold is a rare and costly precious metal, frankincense is symbolic of holiness and righteousness, and myrrh is a natural gum or resin extracted from the same small, thorny tree that was present at Jesus's death and burial.) From Jesus's birth to His physical death, words such as *rare, precious, costly, holy, righteous,* and *divine* describe the One who bore the crown of thorns.

When we are sensitive to the stirring of the Holy Spirit, we become more aware that God is always at work in our lives in both big and small ways. Like the friend who invited me to Community Bible Study, God is always inviting us forward in faith, teaching us, calling us, and equipping us along the way. God perfectly wove my path from a lonely stay-at-home mom, to a playgroup, to a life-changing ministry that helps me dive deep into His Word, thereby unleashing my gifts of teaching and writing.

With Joseph and Mary, God used an unsuspecting visit from the Magi to prepare their hearts for the next detour in life. It was a merciful gesture, followed by a divine warning for the sake of preserving the destiny of this sacred family. While human wisdom usually comes with age and experience, godly wisdom comes when we open our eyes and our minds to the One listening and leading from above.

Perhaps Paul, one of the wisest Jewish men of his day, and a faithful disciple of Christ, says it best in 1 Corinthians 2:3–5 (ESV):

> And I was with you in weakness and in fear and much trembling, and my speech and my message were not in plausible words of wisdom, but in demonstration of the Spirit and of power, so that your faith might not rest in the wisdom of men but in the power of God.

Faith in God cannot rest solely in the knowledge of Him. Faith must rest in knowing Him, personally and powerfully.

PRAYER

Lord, help us not be wise in our own eyes, but be transformed by the renewing of our minds in your power and your infinite wisdom. Lead us, like the wise men, to a face-to-face encounter with You, the Light of the World. May we be changed through Your Word and choose the narrow way home to the Father. In Jesus's name. Amen.

CHAPTER TEN

When God Calls You Back to Egypt

As for you, you meant evil against me, but God
meant it for good, to bring about that many people
should be kept alive, as they are today.

—*Genesis 50:20* ESV

In all its splendor and truth, Christmas is a most joyous time of year. The incarnation of the infant Savior itself is a miracle replete with the tender mercy and sacrificial love of God to send Emmanuel for us, to live with us, and ultimately within us. The incarnation is why we need to celebrate the spirit of Christmas all year round. However, when December rolls around, I have been known to say out loud that it just doesn't seem fair that Christmas, making room for Him and celebrating His birth, should have to find its own room in the midst of shopping, end-of-year tax planning, parties, financial stress, flu season, and shorter hours of sunlight. There have been years I wished the traditional calendar was different.

Could we celebrate Christmas in July? Maybe it's not a bad idea, because immediately following the hustle and bustle of Christmas comes the New Year's reminder of extra pounds and lighter bank accounts. Bah humbug! Just as we slow down, dig deep, and discover the joy of the first coming of Christ all over again, we wake up to a new year and old habits of guilt and shame over increased weight and insufficient funds. Perhaps you can relate?

I suffered from an eating disorder during some critical years of identity formation and body image conception. After Jesus delivered me from the bondage of bulimia, I realized I was still functioning with a distorted view of my body and an unhealthy relationship with food. As an athlete, I had always held the image of a muscular, lean figure in high esteem, as if it were an idol to worship and emulate. Although God had delivered me from my "Egypt" (the bondage of slavery to bulimia), the consequences of years of skewed thinking and unrealistic personal expectations left me anxious. I still worried about my weight, my body image, and the difficulty of learning to be comfortable in my own skin. Mix an unrealistic expectation about body image with a holiday like Christmas, filled with food, drink, and more food, and you have a believer who is tempted to return to her old ways and old coping mechanisms.

Each December Satan tries to steal my joy by tempting me to focus on myself, my sins, and my struggles, and not on Jesus. For example, I struggle with hospitality. Cooking is not one of my gifts, and in my mind, hospitality has always been associated with food and the temptation to overindulge. These could become good excuses to never invite anyone over for dinner, or they could become opportunities to fully rely on God to lead me to a great, easy recipe. More importantly, I could try to find a way out of the temptation (1 Cor. 10:13). Although God has freed me from the grip of bulimia, Satan still tries to tempt me to return to my old habits and buy into the lies created by my erroneous thinking.

During Advent, as I try to make more room in my life for Christ, I'm always tempted to fill the void with food, drink, stuff, and more stuff. Then I wake up in January promising to do better and be better—hoping for real change in the new year and resolving to try harder. Perhaps you have experienced a similar type of post-Christmas blues and a January resolve to do better. Maybe your struggle isn't with food but with strained relationships within your family, or the grief of missing a loved one who has died. The problem is when we start trying to do better or be better by our own resolve and in our own strength. We can miss the blessing of Advent, the blessing of making room for Him, and the benefits of hopefully waiting on the hand of God to move and direct us into a new year, a new hope, and a new way of thinking.

In Matthew chapter 2, we read how Joseph and Mary experienced the first Advent after the wise men departed. The passage following the traditional Christmas story continues Mary's faith journey, while also demonstrating God's sovereignty as the Master Weaver of creation, time, space, and prophecy. If we aren't careful, we will end the Christmas story with the departure of the wise men, box up our nativity scenes, and fail to see the literary genius, prophetic providence, and protective hand of God intervene in a most spectacular way in the lives of Joseph, Mary, and Jesus. So as you pack up your own nativity set this year, I encourage you to reflect on the verses following the Christmas story. Discover the blessing and benefit of the hand of God as He moves in believers who desire to make room for the first and, ultimately, the second coming of Christ.

Matthew 2:13–23 records the sacred family's flight to Egypt prior to a prophetic settlement in Nazareth. The layers of God's love, mercy, and faithfulness for Joseph, Mary, and Jesus within these verses are almost too intricate to sift through and comprehend. This passage contains a *trifecta* of prophecies, not to men-

tion God's providence and protection. After the wise men departed, God sent another angel to Joseph in a dream, directing him to
take the reins of fatherhood and husbandhood in hand and flee to
Egypt with his bride and his newborn. Joseph got to be the heroic
leader and protector of his family, following a troublesome start to
marriage and parenting. Perhaps God understood Joseph needed
this boost, and He provided it in a most precarious way.

The very wise men who fell to their knees in worship and adoration of Jesus became the messengers who inadvertently initiated
a death sentence from the courts of King Herod to the children of
Bethlehem. Jeremiah's painful prophecy was fulfilled: "A voice is
heard in Ramah, mourning and great weeping, Rachel weeping for
her children refusing to be comforted, because they are no more"
(Jer. 31:15). Nevertheless, what Herod meant for evil God used for
good to protect Jesus and His parents and to fulfill His plan for all
humanity.

The same God who brought the Israelites *out* of Egypt to
protect them from the final plague—the death of every firstborn
child—was now sending Jesus and His parents *into* Egypt to protect God's firstborn child from a jealous ruler. Egypt, a land that
once held God's people in bondage and slavery, was transformed
into a refuge for the future King of Kings to grow and thrive under
the protection of His earthly father and mother. Fullfilling Hosea's
prophecy, God would eventually call His Son out of Egypt, just as
God calls each and every one of us out of our own Egypt of bondage to Himself through the life, death, and resurrection of Jesus.

Another angel appeared to Joseph in a dream, telling him it
was safe to return home, "But when he heard that Archelaus was
reigning over Judea in place of his father Herod, he was afraid to go
there, and being warned in a dream he withdrew to the district of
Galilee" (Mt. 2:22 HCSB). Joseph was no different than the desert
Israelites moving with the cloud. When God sent an angel, Joseph
moved likewise. He knew it wasn't safe to stay where they currently
were, and God confirmed it, thereby fulfilling another prophecy

that Jesus would be called a Nazarene (Matt. 2:23). God master-fully wove our ability to think, reason, and discern into His plan, providence, and provision of a Savior.

These verses do contain some amazing fulfillments of prophecy, mind-boggling parallels to the Old Testament, and God's sovereign usage of foreshadowing and irony. They turn our thinking upside down and inside out, but we must be careful not to romanticize these verses. Matthew chapter 2, like all of Scripture, contains real people with real experiences, feelings, and fears. I can only imagine what was going through Mary's mind as she left Bethlehem. She had come on a donkey, then she left on a donkey, holding her baby in her arms instead of in her womb. Egypt was a long journey, but Joseph and Mary fled in faith—faith in the message of God delivered by an angel and faith in His Word to flee, and faith to trust in the unknown once again.

The faith of Joseph and Mary astounds me. Every time I read these verses I want to cheer for Joseph's immediate obedience and bold leadership, as well as Mary's humble submission to God and to her husband. Matthew 2:14 (ESV) says Joseph "rose and took the child and his mother by night and departed to Egypt." Following the angelic warning, Joseph immediately arose, gathered his family, and departed during the dark hours of night, heeding God's Word and trusting His protection and provision. When God calls you into a time of darkness, your faith becomes the only light you need to illuminate His Will and His Way. Joseph and Mary were fleeing in faith—not away from God, but directly into the center of His will for a season in Egypt.

During the first coming of Christ, Joseph and Mary made room for Jesus in their hearts, their home, their lives, and their minds. With space for God to move and work, Joseph and Mary were able to receive God's merciful warning and respond in faith instead of fear. A logical man would have departed in the daylight when danger was visible and direction was clear, yet a man who knows the love and promises of God will depart on command, even when the danger is unknown and the destination unclear. And a woman like Mary, who has faith in the same God as her man, will follow him even when it leads into the darkness of the unknown.

As I read and study these Scriptures, I find myself asking, "Hadn't Mary and Joseph been through enough? Hadn't they endured more than their fair share of ridicule, confusion, and hardship?" After growing up as a child of divorced parents, enduring bulimia, suffering from a dream-altering running injury, surviving a dark season of depression, struggling as a new wife and mother, losing a loved one too soon, and living daily with a certain level of anxiety, sometimes I want to cry out to God, "Haven't I been through enough? God, when does the pain and struggle end? When does the relief come?" Have you ever asked God similar questions about your own life?

It takes a certain type of courage to ask God these tough questions. We see this courage in Mary and Joseph as they trusted God and fled to Egypt for the sake of preserving the life of the Giver of Life. Perhaps after the birth of Jesus, the shepherd's visit, the temple dedication experience, and the visit by the Magi, Joseph and Mary just wanted to go home to a place that was comfortable and familiar. But God called them to a place that was far from their comfort zone, a place where centuries earlier God had demonstrated His great love, mercy, and power to deliver His people from danger.

At times God has called me back to my own Egypt for the purpose of reminding me of his redemptive love and His power to deliver me from bondage. As I spend time sifting through memories of my childhood and the years of enduring an eating disorder, God not only shows me just how far He has brought me, He also reveals deeper layers of sin and struggle. Setting me free and healing several areas of brokenness allowed God to show me some of the less obvious issues in my life, like the underlying current of worry and anxiety.

Just as He did for Mary and Joseph, when God calls us back to Egypt, He does it for our good, for our protection and preservation, and to teach us full dependence on Him. It's not an easy journey of faith to have to revisit our past struggles and sins. But when we commit to the journey through faith, we can believe that what Satan means for evil God will work out for good. Like Mary and Joseph with the light of Christ illuminating their path to Egypt, when we cry out to God, "Haven't I been through enough?" we can remember His plan is always leading us into the center of His will. Instead of running from our past, we can flee to God in faith, claiming Philippians 1:6: "that he who began a good work in you will carry it on to completion until the day of Christ Jesus." God made a way out of Egypt for the Israelites through the Red Sea, and in His timing He called His one and only Son out of Egypt. Likewise, we can trust that He will make a way out of slavery, sin, and temptation for you and me. Jesus helps us put our "Egypt" in the rearview mirror.

PRAYER

Merciful God, give us the faith to fully trust and depend on You. May we possess the courage, like Mary and Joseph, to obediently go when You call us to dark, difficult places. Free us from our Egypt—those areas of sin that keep us in bondage—and use those areas to reveal more of Your plan and purpose in our lives. In Jesus's name. Amen.

CHAPTER ELEVEN

When the Lamb Becomes the Good Shepherd

*For the Lamb in the midst of the throne will be their
shepherd, and he will guide them to springs of living
water, and God will wipe away
every tear from their eyes.*

—Revelation 7:17 (ESV)

June 11, 2011 was a day some people called me a hero, but on
that day God, through His grace, called my husband and me to
our knees, facedown in humility. Following the last day of school,
it was our family tradition to celebrate the beginning of summer
break with a day at the pool. My husband Patrick and I, along with
our three young children (ages nine, six, and three at the time),
invited another family with young children to join us. We rested
poolside in the warm sun, chatting with friends against the back-

drop of children splashing, playing, and laughing. We welcomed the change from months of packing lunches, helping with homework, and waiting in the pickup line. The balmy rays of the sun contrasted with the chilly pool water, energizing our tired bodies after a busy year of school. It was the exhale I had been longing for since winter, until the unthinkable happened and nearly knocked the life out of me.

As a mother of three, I usually have my mommy radar on, especially around water. I recall scanning the pool frequently that day to account for all the children, before turning my attention to my friends to chat and catch up. As we conversed about our busy lives, I remember experiencing an unsettling feeling in my spirit as I turned to scan the pool again. I counted off Jacob and Samantha, my two oldest children, then our friends' children—but not Daniel, my youngest child. Daniel had been playing at the pool steps just a few feet from me, jumping in the shallow end with his swim tube around his waist only minutes before.

I jumped to my feet and called to my husband, "Where is Daniel?" Hoping I had just missed spotting him behind a pool chair, I turned to the shallow end of the pool. There at the base of the steps, lying facedown three feet under water, was my three-year-old little boy.

I screamed his name like only a mother can, yelled for my husband to call 911, and then jumped what felt like ten feet to my baby boy. I scooped Daniel out of the water. His eyes were closed, and his face and lips had begun to turn blue. God switched me, a medical professional, into clinical mode. My worst fear, panic, and hysteria were put on hold, so a clinician could work on her patient. The next few minutes were unbelievably surreal as I began administering rescue breaths. Desperately giving breaths, and not taking my eyes off his face, I could hear everything around me clearly. Another mother at the pool was already on her cell phone with 911, a nearby male voice was telling me Daniel had a pulse, and my friend was praying, "Jesus, please, Jesus, Lord Jesus, help him."

Soon I felt each breath reach the depths of his lungs. His eyelids began to open, and color returned to his lips. I diligently gave more and more breaths, and then Daniel locked eyes with me. Then he began to cry—scared, helpless, and fearful. The clinician in me waited a moment, then the mother in me picked him up and rocked him back and forth.

Patrick reached down to embrace his son. I slowly rose to my feet in shock, my face in my hands as if my head might spontaneously combust with emotion. As my hands parted from my tear-filled eyes, I caught a glimpse of all the other children grouped together, all eyes focused on me, as if waiting for me to say something. In that pivotal moment, the Holy Spirit gave me the words, and I said, "He's okay, he's going to be fine." Then I turned to catch up with my husband in the parking lot to meet the ambulance.

The hours and days that followed were a humbling, stomach-churning, emotional roller coaster for our family. At the hospital, Daniel vomited pool water for several hours and color did not return to his face until the next morning. The doctors called it a near-drowning but told us that very little water had actually entered his lungs. I learned that babies and small children have a reflex that closes off their trachea when they are submerged in cold water. It's called the Mammalian Reflex—designed by God, named by man. This reflex may have bought us the time we needed to respond. As I lay next to Daniel in his little hospital bed, I watched and listened to him breathe, too anxious to sleep. My husband told me later that he stood over the two of us for hours that night while we slept, with tears in his eyes, thanking God for His mercy and grace in what He had done through me.

Joseph and Mary also experienced a day filled with fear and panic when they lost track of their Son Jesus on the journey home from Jerusalem to Nazareth. Similar to our family's experience at the pool, this was a day after which Joseph and Mary would never be the same. Luke 2:41–52 tells about the experience of humility and grace when they watched their little Lamb become the Good Shepherd.

Luke 2:41–42 (ESV) says, "Now his parents went to Jerusalem every year at the Feast of the Passover. And when he was twelve years old, they went up according to custom." The Passover is one of three great Jewish festivals celebrating the time during Egyptian captivity when God Himself passed over the blood-marked homes of the Israelites, sparing their firstborn children (Ex. 12). According to Jewish tradition, all males were required to attend this annual eight-day festival (also referred to as the Feast of Unleavened Bread) in Jerusalem. Perhaps Mary's presence on this journey in Luke chapter 2 illustrates the close bond she had with Joseph and Jesus. The approximately seventy-mile trek from Nazareth to Jerusalem was challenging with a family, and scholars believe it would have been a five-day journey on foot, with Jewish families usually traveling in large groups with other relatives. Since the younger folks usually mingled during the day, and immediate families would come back together later in the evening to pitch their tents at night, this explains why Joseph and Mary could go a day's journey before they discovered Jesus was missing.

Luke 2:43 (ESV) says, "And when the feast was ended, as they were returning, the boy Jesus stayed behind in Jerusalem. His parents did not know it." Can you imagine the crescendo of panic in Mary's and Joseph's hearts as they realized their little Lamb, now twelve years old, was missing? Perhaps their conversation sounded something like this: "Where did Jesus go? How could we have lost him?" "Mary, I thought you were watching him." "No, Joseph, I told you to keep an eye on him!" Can you imagine the fear, anxiety, propensity to blame, and outright terror they experienced, as no one had any information on Jesus's whereabouts? I wonder if Mary could even pray in those moments? Or did she feel such an overwhelming sense of guilt for losing track of Jesus that she wanted to hide from God and everyone else? Did they pitch their tent that night, or did they start the day's journey back up the hill in the dark to find their lost Lamb?

Scripture tells us that after three days of searching they finally found Him back in Jerusalem, in the temple. Three days. *Can you imagine?* Three days was a number with a sacred significance, for Jesus's disciples, followers, and His own mother would endure three days of grief after His death on a cross. Three agonizing days must have felt like three years to a mother and father who longed to see their Son's face, hear his laugh, and feel his warm embrace.

Mary and Joseph retraced their steps back to the temple, only to be astonished by what and who they found! Right there in the midst of the rabbis and teachers was Jesus, their twelve-year-old boy turned pupil of the Law. Scripture says Jesus was listening and asking questions, a technique often used in Jewish teaching to engage others in meaningful learning and exchange of information. Jesus wasn't teaching that day, but those in earshot were amazed and astonished by His knowledge and understanding.

Developmental psychologist Jean Piaget proposed that children develop more abstract reasoning skills as part of their last stage of development, usually between the ages of eleven and sixteen. Abstract thinking is defined as the ability to think about objects, principles, and ideas that are not physically present. At twelve years old, Jesus understood the eternal concept that Nazareth was not His home, and that God's plan and purpose for His life was much greater than what anyone else could imagine. Most kids lose their minds when they hit puberty, around age twelve, but Jesus seemed to have found His!

Mary's initial reaction after three emotionally and physically exhausting days of searching for her Son demonstrated her authenticity as a mother. She was raw with emotion. Mary said to Jesus in front of everyone in the temple that day, "Son, why have you treated us so? Behold, your father and I have been searching for you in great distress" (Lk. 2:48 ESV).

Momma wasn't happy, and when momma's not happy, we all know how that usually goes. To say Mary was upset would be putting it mildly. Mary was most likely functioning on pure adrenaline, a byproduct of fear and panic. Mary even may have been tempted to snatch Jesus up by His tunic and march His wise tail outside the temple! Her response is organic and unrefined, a condition I can appreciate as a mother.

H.A.L.T. is an acronym used in Alcoholics Anonymous and other addiction rehab programs that serves as a reminder to those tempted by past addictions to be careful when they feel hungry, angry, lonely, or tired. Mary was most likely all of these. Her visceral reaction reflected a mother's fear of experiencing the worst pain imaginable, the loss of a child. Mary said to Jesus, "How could you do this to me? Don't scare me like this! How could you make me feel this way? I don't want to feel this way!" Fear can make us self-protective, and pain can make us selfish, because we feel these emotions so deeply. Praise God that faith is not a feeling. Faith is a choice. In the aftermath of a parent's worst nightmare, Mary came to a fork in the road and had to choose the state of mind in which she would return home: the way of fear or the way of faith.

Jesus's answer to His parent's question regarding His whereabouts indicates His understanding of God's plan. "Why were you looking for me? Did you not know that I must be in my Father's house?" Other translations (KJV, MSG) relay the idea that Jesus "must be about his Father's business" or "dealing with the things of his Father." Interestingly, these telling questions were Jesus's first recorded words in Scripture. Jesus did not seem fazed by His mother's emotional response; rather, He very matter-of-factly answered her with conviction and purpose. He was now accountable to God, His Father, and God alone. However, out of His great love for His earthly parents, and as a model of obedience, Scripture says He returned to Nazareth and was submissive to them as He grew in wisdom and stature, and in favor with God and man.

Perhaps Mary and Joseph did not fully understand their Son's response, yet they caught a glimpse of Jesus's calling and purpose that day in the temple, just as had been prophesied twelve years earlier through Simeon and Anna. Prior to this day, Mary had pondered and treasured the words of an angel, shepherds, wise men, and prophets. Hereafter she would treasure in her heart the words of her own Son Jesus, the Lamb that would soon become the Good Shepherd. For Mary, it was like hearing other people tell you that Jesus loves you your whole life, until one day you open the Bible and begin to hear Jesus speak directly to your heart.

Romans 10:17 says, "So faith comes from hearing, and hearing through the word of Christ." While losing Jesus for three days was another one of God's merciful ways of preparing Mary for Jesus's destiny on the cross, God began speaking directly to Mary through the words of Jesus. And just as her child grew in stature and favor with God, perhaps Mary's faith grew in depth and knowledge of God's plan and Jesus's ultimate role in her life. Faith grows through repetition of the truth. Mary had pondered and treasured truth from several other sources, but now she treasured learning truth from Jesus Himself. "And the Word became flesh and dwelt among us" (John 1:14 ESV).

God used a frightening experience to teach Mary and Joseph more about Jesus. Likewise, almost losing our son brought my husband and me to a screeching halt, down on our knees with broken spirits and contrite hearts. These sacrifices are holy and pleasing to God (Ps. 51:17) and this is also the place, like Mary experienced with Jesus, where we come to a fork in the road. Fear or faith?

Pain has a way of making us either more selfish and fearful, or more humble and faithful. We get to choose. We can respond to our pain by withdrawing into ourselves, attempting to cope, or lashing out in selfish defense. Or we can allow our pain to humble us and bring us to our knees to receive God's love, grace, and mercy. We know our son Daniel is still with us today, not because of any heroics, but because it was not God's will to take him. By the grace and mercy of God, I was merely the vessel He used to breathe life-saving breaths into Daniel's body.

The panic and subsequent pain of this "what if" moment could have left me paralyzed and angry at God. And, honestly, for a little while it did. Perhaps similar to Mary, I asked God some bold questions like "Why did you let this happen?" and "Why would you do this to me?" The thought of what if Daniel had drowned in the pool that day was overwhelming. However, until I allowed myself to face the terrible question of "what if," God would not ask me the most difficult question of my life. After enough time had passed and some of my raw emotions had developed protective scabs, I surrendered to the horrific thought of what if Daniel had died. In the midst of this surrender, in my broken, humbled spirit, God asked me, "Would you still love me if Daniel had drowned?" It was a question I couldn't answer at first. It was a question in merciful preparation of events to come in my life, revealing it was God's turn to perform some spiritual CPR on me.

For months after my son's near-drowning, I was overcome with anxious thoughts about anything and everything bad that *might* happen. One of the most anxiety-provoking experiences was a re-curring dream about almost drowning in a lake, much like the one I grew up on. Although I could never recall the whole dream, I always remembered the part when I was sinking lower and lower into the depths of the dark water, only to look up and realize I was in too deep to swim back up to the light of the surface. Then I would wake up in a cold-sweat, gasping for breath, perplexed at such a disturbing visual.

One day in church when we sang "How He Loves," by the David Crowder Band, God revealed to me a life-changing truth by connecting that song to my vivid dream. As I sang the lyrics that compared God's grace to an ocean in which we were sinking, the tears began to stream down my face. God, in His mercy, was invit-ing me to sink, as if to drown in surrender to His grace, and to trust that He would provide the very breath I need to live, if I would only surrender and stop trying to fight my way to the surface.

Anxious thoughts had consumed me my whole life. From an early age they had driven my need to perform, resulting in a perfectionist who tried to control her own destiny. But God used one of the most anxiety-provoking events of my life to lift me out of such erroneous thinking and draw me into His grace. My life verse is 2 Corinthians 12:9: "My grace is sufficient for you, for my power is made perfect in weakness." While singing "How He Loves," I realized that until I truly experienced God's grace, I couldn't truly experience His love. That day I resolved to stop fighting anxiety on my own and trust that God's grace is enough.

Similar to Mary's experience, my son's near-drowning was an event God used for my three "little lambs" to teach me about having a childlike faith. Luke 18:16–17 (ESV) says, "But Jesus called them to him, saying, 'Let the children come to me, and do not hinder them, for to such belongs the kingdom of God. Truly, I say to you, whoever does not receive the kingdom of God like a child shall not enter it.'" Humility is most definitely caught, not taught, and each one of my children reflected the humble faith of a child following this traumatic experience.

When Jacob, my oldest, realized the crisis unfolding at the pool, he told me he began praying with the belief that mommy may not be able to fix it, but Jesus can. When I told the group of children that Daniel was going to be okay, my middle child Sami told me she never doubted but believed that what her mother spoke was truth. Daniel's demonstration of faith is perhaps the sweetest. His favorite Bible story was Daniel and the Lion's Den, because in his precious (then three-year-old) mind, he *was* that Daniel. Still to this day he tells me, "God saved me, Mommy. God saved me." And I can look at him and say, "Yes, Son, God did save you!" This mother's prayer is that all my children will one day confess with their mouths and believe in their hearts that Jesus Christ is Savior and Lord and that I can truly say, "I have no greater joy than to hear that my children are walking in the truth" (3 Jn. 1:4).

Perhaps you have experienced a traumatic event or painful loss that left you shaken and waffling between fear and faith. Maybe you struggle with being angry at God over your own "what if" questions. Are you paralyzed with fear or anxious thoughts, yet you desire to walk in faith? I encourage you, like Mary, to ponder and treasure the words of Christ in the midst of life's storms and struggles. Instead of trying to cope or self-protect, allow your pain to humble you and bring you to your knees, into a posture to receive God's grace, mercy, and everlasting love. As you spend time reading, praying, and pondering Scripture, allow the Lamb of God to become your Good Shepherd—always protecting, always leading you gently down the path of faith, and always pursuing you when you stray from the fold.

PRAYER

Good Shepherd, You are the way, the truth, and the life, and no one comes to the Father except through faith in You, Jesus. Help us to choose faith when fear wants to lead us astray. Mercifully extend your Shepherd's crook that points us in the direction of truth and help us to live with a child-like faith. In Jesus's name. Amen.

CHAPTER TWELVE

Mary, Did You Know? The Power of Uncontaminated Faith

His mother said to the servants, "Do whatever he tells you."

—*John 2:5* NIV

For many, the passing of a loved one marks a significant turning point, after which they never view life quite the same. Personally, this shift in my focus occurred after the passing of my grandfather. He was known as Granddaddy. A faithful husband, war veteran, father of eight children, and grandfather to nineteen grandchildren, he was a devout Christian and the spiritual patriarch of his large family.

Summers spent with our extended family at my grandparent's home near Jacksonville Beach, Florida, are some of my fondest memories as a child. Granddaddy reminded me of Billy Graham, a preacher he both respected and admired. He was always talking to us about the importance of Jesus in our lives and getting us to memorize Scripture before we could go play at the beach. The grandchildren called this community "Grandmommy's Beach," but we all knew it was Granddaddy who led the march toward Christ in his home, church, and community.

Even though my grandmother went home to be with the Lord several years before my grandfather, it wasn't until Granddaddy became ill that God began to speak to my heart about the importance of leaving a legacy of faith within a family. I admired his consistent message of faith. He was in the Word every day. His conversations somehow found their way back to Jesus, he sang (albeit out of tune) hymns and spiritual songs as he went about his day, and his greatest joy was when someone walked down the aisle at church and received Christ as their Savior.

When he went into hospice, I experienced a deep conviction in my spirit to pass the torch of faith, so to speak, to those in our extended family who were willing to run the race. A few days before my grandfather died, I walked the aisle at my own church and knelt at the altar to pray an "Isaiah-like" prayer. "Here I am, Lord. Send me to carry the torch of faith and run the race that my grandfather can no longer sustain." In honor of my grandparents, especially my grandfather, I committed to both living and leaving a legacy of faith for my own children, and hopefully my grandchildren, just as my grandparents had done for me.

Although the passing of a grandparent is much different than the loss of a spouse, Mary may have experienced a similar feeling when her beloved Joseph passed away, leaving her a widow and single mother. Scripture does not reveal when or how Joseph died, however, finding Jesus in the temple with the other rabbis is the last mention of Joseph in Scripture. Scholars believe that Joseph died sometime between Jesus's adolescence at age twelve and the beginning of His ministry at approximately thirty. Regardless of the details of his passing, Mary must have grieved her loss through countless tears, much prayer, deep soul-searching, and a more dependent relationship with her children, especially Jesus. Perhaps Joseph's death was a significant turning point, after which she never viewed life or her purpose quite the same way again.

After Mary and Joseph's departure from the temple with Jesus, the next time we find Mary in Scripture is in John 2:1–12, at a wedding in Cana. Although her recorded words are few, they are mighty words of faith in her Son, God's Son, Jesus, in whom all things are possible. Three days after calling His first disciples, Jesus, Mary, and the disciples attended a wedding in Cana, during which the wine had run out. Mary informed Jesus of the absence of wine, yet He responded, "Woman, what does this have to do with me? My hour has not yet come."

Mary then told the servants, "Do whatever He tells you." Jesus instructed them to fill six stone jars with water and serve some to the master of the feast who, after tasting the water turned wine, inquired of the bridegroom why he saved the good wine until later. This was Jesus's first miracle, about which the apostle John said, "manifested his glory," and "his disciples believed in him" (Jn. 2:11).

The relational dynamics between Jesus and Mary in these verses is precious. Jesus's initial response to Mary was, in essence: "Dear woman, it's not my time; don't put me to the test. Trust God's timing." Faith never puts demands on God. Nevertheless, Mary's bold response to Jesus's words, although directed toward the servants, was in support of Him: "Do whatever He tells you, because He can do anything!" As the wine ran dry, Mary's excitement bubbled over. She demonstrated an uncontaminated faith in Jesus and His ability to provide exactly what was needed. Despite Mary's ill-timed request of her Son, Jesus honored Mary's faith in Him out of His great love for her and proceeded to miraculously turn water into wine. Following a time in Mary's life when she lost the love of her life, Joseph, and possibly her hope and security for the future, a time when perhaps only faith remained, we find Mary publicly demonstrating absolute faith in Jesus at a wedding, symbolic of hope and love.

1 Corinthians 13:13 (NLT) states, "Three things will last forever—faith, hope, and love—and the greatest of these is love." Woven throughout the story of the wedding at Cana, we find themes of faith, hope, and love intertwined like a triple-braided cord. First of all, Jesus's public ministry and His first miracle in Scripture occurred at this wedding on the third day after calling His first disciples, foreshadowing the miracle of the resurrection, and symbolic of our eternal hope in Christ. Jesus's first miracle taking place at a wedding also points toward a future miracle at the Marriage Supper of the Lamb, when all God's children will gather at the table in eternal communion with God, a symbol of God's great love and the completion of His salvation plan through Jesus Christ.

The six jars that Jesus told the servants to fill were primarily used as purification jars, yet once He turned the water into wine they became symbolic of the blood Jesus would ultimately sacrifice to purify us once and for all. Therefore, out of His great love for us, Jesus Himself became the seventh jar, a number symbolic of perfection and completion. In this first miracle, Jesus provided an abundance of wine but gave the bridegroom all the credit. Jesus is the ultimate bridegroom, and His church is the bride—a relationship built on faith, hope, and love. Furthermore, by turning water into better wine than was served to the guests initially, Jesus symbolized His eternal glory that will be manifest in the last days. And lastly, because of Mary's demonstration of uncontaminated faith, the disciples believed in Him and began their own journeys of faith with Christ.

Mary's actions and words in John 2 indicate that this was the day she knew that Jesus could do anything in accordance to the will of God. Despite her difficult circumstances as a widow and a single mother, thus carrying the torch of faith for her family, Mary demonstrated 1 Timothy 1:5 (MSG): "Simply love—love uncontaminated by self-interest and counterfeit faith, a life open to God."

Uncontaminated faith sets us free to hope in the eternal and experience God's love in the now. While Mary's journey of faith hadn't been easy, God demonstrated His love, faithfulness, and merciful provision and brought her to a place of complete trust and surrender to His plan. Perhaps this was the day Mary set aside her own plans and desires and set her Son free to fulfill God's plan, minister to the world, and save lost souls, despite the cost to Him and to her.

After my grandfather died, I thought a lot about what it means to live and leave a legacy of faith. Perhaps you have similar questions about how to live a life of faith. The Bible defines faith in Hebrews 11:1. "Now faith is the assurance of things hoped for, the conviction of things not seen." But what exactly does this verse mean? What does it look like to live out your faith on a mundane Monday or a wacky Wednesday? Or the day your world turns upside down, and life as you know it will never be the same?

Perhaps Mary is an ideal person to emulate when it comes to living a life of faith. While her journey of faith began the moment she said yes to Jesus, she has shown us that faith is an ever-winding journey, not necessarily a destination. In fact, as a result of the salvation we have available through Jesus, faith is an eternal journey with Christ that beckons us to begin before it is too late.

Through the power of the Holy Spirit, Mary conceived a baby who ultimately saved her soul. Salvation comes by grace through faith, and we are each invited on this journey. God chose Mary to give birth to Jesus—God incarnate—because we cannot save ourselves. Faith is like a gift that waits patiently under the Christmas tree to be discovered, unwrapped, and cherished as the means to a relationship with our heavenly Father.

Mary's life demonstrates that faith is also mutually exclusive. Just as a tossed coin can never land on both heads and tails, faith can never share space with any opposing force. Faith takes up the whole space that it fills, leaving no room for doubt, no room for fear, and no room for anything that could contaminate its power to rescue and save. Mary also demonstrates that faith is believing in Jesus regardless of the outcome, in the presence or the absence of a miracle. Faith uncontaminated by the world is believing that Hope and Love is a Person, not a feeling. And a cord of three strands (faith, hope, and love) is never easily broken (Eccl. 4:12).

Mary's life, similar to my grandfather's, also demonstrates that faith is consistent when built on the foundation of Jesus Christ, with hope as its anchor. At the wedding in Cana, Mary boldly demonstrated an assurance of things hoped for and her conviction of things not seen when she turned to Jesus in faith, believing that He could do anything. As we continue to follow Mary toward the cross, we will see that uncontaminated faith is following Jesus, despite the cost, in the presence or the absence of a miracle.

Is there someone in your life whose faith has inspired you? Perhaps you have a family member whose legacy of faith lives on in your family tree. Do you desire to live and leave your own legacy of faith for your loved ones? I invite you to ponder someone whose life of faith has inspired you. How might you apply their influence in your own life? Allow Mary's journey and her uncontaminated faith in Jesus to encourage you as you travel your own path and build your own legacy of faith.

As I reflect on my grandfather's legacy of faith, Mary's journey of faith, and the intimate relationship between faith, hope, and love, I am reminded of 1 Thessalonians 1:2–3: "We give thanks to God always for all of you, constantly mentioning you in our prayers, remembering before our God and Father your work of faith and labor of love and steadfastness of hope in our Lord Jesus Christ." Let us give thanks to those who have gone before us, lived a life of obedience to Christ, and demonstrated the power of uncontaminated faith.

PRAYER

Faithful Father, You have graciously provided the gift of faith so that we may live out a life of obedience to Christ doing, just as Mary directed the servants, whatever He tells us. Thank You for those who have gone before us, both in Scripture and in our families and communities, who have passed down a legacy of faith. Help us to live out a faith, uncontaminated by the world, that will set us free to hope in the eternal and experience God's love in the now. In Jesus's name. Amen.

Chapter Thirteen

True Relationship: When Obedience Is Thicker than Blood

Anyone who does God's will is my brother and sister and mother.

—*Mark 3:34 NLT*

For the first thirty plus years of my life, I relied on the maternal wall of strength that is my mother. She was always my rock, my home base, and my refuge for emotional comfort and stability. Therefore, when my husband and I arrived at the crossroads of marital bliss meets marital reality, I called my mama! I not only called my mama, I cried to my mama, I ran to my mama, and I leaned hard against my maternal wall of support for unceasing love and acceptance. But all that calling and crying and maternal dependency dismayed my husband. By not leaving and cleaving on an emotional level from my family of origin, especially my mother, I robbed my husband of becoming my confidant, and I temporarily cheated God out of the opportunity to work for His glory in our marriage relationship.

In fact, before I was willing to truly leave and cleave and fully invest in my relationship with my husband, there was a time in our marriage when the devil had me convinced that divorce was my best option. During a time when I was knee-deep in diapers, baby food, spit up, three dogs, and a husband who was never home, I bought into the lie: "You are already doing all this by yourself; what do you need him for?" I was like a horse with blinders, pulling the weight of the world, while the deceiver dangled the carrot of divorce in my narrow-minded view. I knew from my childhood experience that divorce was a deep pit with a terrible view, but I was deceived into thinking I would be less miserable without the unmet expectation of my husband's physical presence and help.

Thankfully, God worked my inappropriate, maternal dependency for good. He used my mother, speaking from the pain of her own choice to divorce my father, to remind me that the devil is a liar, a thief, and a master of deception, and that he comes to steal, kill, and destroy. While there are certainly situations in which divorce is warranted, my mother encouraged me to turn to God's Word to help me discern His truth. Satan, using lies to deceive me into thinking that divorce was my best option, wanted more than anything to tempt me into taking the same generational path as my parents.

But God had a different plan. Divorce is a generational sin. It is a pervasive, deceitful lie of our culture. This disease has infected our minds and convinced us that by chopping down and splitting the family tree, we can replant and grow new roots with hopes of bearing the same good fruit. Sadly, that is not the way it usually turns out.

While my relationship with my mother was a healthy and supportive one, my use or abuse of it was not healthy, and that created a blockade for growth in my own family tree. Only by God's grace and mercy did I come to see my unhealthy dependency on my mother, and how it prevented my husband from becoming my most intimate confidant. God helped me stand upright in His strength and establish deep roots of love and trust with my husband, and subsequently our children. Thus, our family tree could grow and begin to bear fruit in the unity of Christ. Leaving your blood relatives and cleaving to your spouse breaks the chains of generational sin. It requires obedience to God's will and a leap of faith into holy matrimony.

Mary's next appearance in Scripture teaches us about leaving and cleaving according to God's will and purpose. Her experience actually occurs in three gospel accounts: Matthew 12, Mark 3, and Luke 8. All these are red-letter prophecies spoken by Christ, a trinity of truth spoken in love from the One who loves us most. We find Jesus leaving His own family of origin in obedience to the will of His Father. We also see Mary letting go of her Son in merciful preparation for meeting her Savior, the bridegroom who awaits His bride. For brevity, allow me to expound on the story as told in Mark. First, let me set the scene and context in which Jesus responds to His own mother and brothers (and sisters, in some translations).

First the Pharisees start false rumors about Jesus being possessed by Satan, which spread far enough to reach Jesus's family. His mother and siblings arrive on the scene, worrying about Jesus and fearing that ". . . he's out of his mind" (Mk. 3:21 NLT). Remember, Mary had released her Son into ministry at the wedding in Cana with one of the simplest yet sweetest statements of faith, but never had she imagined hearing such blasphemy regarding her Son, the long-awaited Messiah. Here are the red letters spoken by Jesus in Mark 3:31–35 (NLT) regarding what the Matthew, Mark, and Luke accounts all designate as "True Family":

Then Jesus's mother and brothers came to see him. They stood outside and sent word for him to come out and talk with them. There was a crowd sitting around Jesus, and someone said, "Your mother and your brothers are outside asking for you." Jesus replied, "Who is my mother? Who are my brothers?" Then he looked at those around him and said, "Look, these are my mother and brothers. Anyone who does God's will is my brother and sister and mother."

The Message Bible renders verses 33–35 in these words:

Jesus responded, "Who do you think are my mother and brothers?" Looking around, taking in everyone seated around him, he said, "Right here, right in front of you— my mother and my brothers. Obedience is thicker than blood. The person who obeys God's will is my brother and sister and mother."

At first glance these verses, spoken indirectly to His mother and siblings who waited outside, may sound cold and somewhat harsh coming from Jesus. His immediate family could not even get a glimpse of Him, due to the large crowd assembled in the home. But perhaps there is a much deeper and richer message beneath the surface. Mary and her family had most likely traveled a long journey to Jerusalem to locate Jesus, and they just wanted to sit down for a long overdue family meeting to find out what in the world was going on and inquire about all the nasty rumors. Access to Jesus was all they longed for. But the messenger returned to the door saying that access had been denied.

Initially it might seem that Jesus was rejecting His family. However, Jesus was *not* denying His blood family—He was denying Himself. And while denying Himself, Jesus was, in fact, *expanding*

His family. In this teachable moment, Jesus was illustrating for all those present, and in the future, what it looks like to live out Matthew 16:24, Mark 8:34, and Luke 9:23. "If anyone would come after me, let him deny himself and take up his cross and follow me."

Is obedience really "thicker than blood"? (Mk. 3:35 MSG). According to Jesus, the answer is yes. Out of obedience to His Father He was taking up His own cross (the salvation of all souls) and following God's will. He was "taking in everyone seated around him" into His forever family. During this critical moment of Jesus's ministry on earth, He gives us a glimpse of what it might look like in our own families to deny ourselves, take up our crosses, and follow Him.

Although Scripture doesn't tell us, I hope that after Jesus demonstrated what the forever family of God looked like, He excused Himself, went outside, and gave His mother a long-awaited holy hug.

Can you imagine Mary standing on the outside looking in, unscathed by the messenger's reply, because as the mother of Christ she knows He is on the inside being true to His name—Jesus, the One who saves? Can you hear Mary gently consoling Jesus's younger brothers and sisters, telling them, "It's okay. He is once again about His Father's business"? Possibly by then Mary had grown accustomed to the surprise factor in her faith walk with Jesus, because He rarely responded, reacted, or revealed the will of the Father in ways that she expected. Perhaps she waited patiently on the outside looking in, trusting that Jesus was at work in a place where she was denied access. Perhaps this was the day Mary witnessed Jesus leaving His family of origin, mercifully preparing her for His journey to the cross. As Jesus expanded His family to include all believers obedient to God's will, it's possible Mary returned home with an expanded understanding of God's will for His Son.

For many, the word *family* carries with it the weight of the world, either in the best sense or the worst sense. Perhaps your family means everything to you, or perhaps the thought of family conjures up emotions of hurt and pain. I can relate to both experiences, but one thing is always true when it comes to family—they are undeniable. Someone birthed you into this world and someone helped raise you and someone still calls you family, even if you don't reciprocate the sentiment. Your family of origin may have all passed away. For others, your family members may be dead to you relationally. Nevertheless, from the beginning of time God ordained the family unit as a reflection of the Trinitarian relationship (Father, Son, and Holy Spirit). The church body, people groups, nations, and civilizations all have their being in His Creation.

Family is the basic battle unit. God's design for true family is echoed throughout Scripture from Genesis to Revelation. God the Father designed family as our training ground for true relationship with Him, His Son, and His Holy Spirit.

Even healthy relationships within a family can translate into an unhealthy dependency, as was the case in my family of origin. Praise God, the words of Jesus recorded by Mark hold the keys to breaking the strongholds of generational sin. They rescue us from the temptation of familial idolatry and help us leave our family of origin and cleave to our new family. Like most fathers, God wants us to obey Him—not out of obligation but out of love, respect, and honor for who He is. In the Old Testament God speaks through the prophet Hosea (6:6): "For I desire steadfast love and not sacrifice, the knowledge of God rather than burnt offerings." These words are echoed by Jesus in the New Testament in Matthew chapters 9 and 12.

Obedience can be thicker than blood only when we are walking in faith. Faith in God and His infinite character have the power to drive a personal obedience that can break any chain of generational sin and mend any tear in family relationships. This includes the family of faith. Jesus's death, burial, and resurrection conquered the power of sin and death over human creation. Jesus expanded His family in these gospel accounts, because He desires to "take in everyone seated around him" into His forever family. He invites all to come and share a place at the family dinner table.

Through the person of Jesus Christ, God wants us to know Him, and thereby love Him more and more, as we enter into an authentic relationship by faith and walk in obedience to His will. When we are walking in obedience to the whispers and nudges of the Spirit of Christ who dwells within us, we will have the gift of discernment regarding dysfunctional family dynamics and unhealthy cycles of generational sin. He will give us a supernatural ability to draw a boundary line where none has existed before.

Listen as God Himself speaks to Moses in Exodus 34:6–7:

The LORD passed before him and proclaimed, "The LORD, the LORD, a God merciful and gracious, slow to anger, and abounding in steadfast love and faithfulness, keeping steadfast love for thousands, forgiving iniquity and transgression and sin, but who will by no means clear the guilty, visiting the iniquity of the fathers on the children and the children's children, to the third and the fourth generation."

God describes Himself, His character, and His infinite desire to forgive in this passage, but "by no means" will He tolerate unrepentant sin generation after generation. Sin leaves a legacy that will be passed down, without the saving grace and forgiving hand of our heavenly Father.

Do you struggle with generational sins or difficult family dynamics? Perhaps you've had trouble leaving your own family of origin and cleaving to your spouse. Is your marriage one of holy matrimony? Are there areas of your life in which you struggle with obedience and wish you had more faith? I encourage you to take some time to ponder how your family of origin may influence you and your thinking, both positively and negatively. Then, as my mother advised, turn to God's Word to help you discern the truth from any lies Satan may use to deceive you and keep you from a true, authentic relationship with God.

As children of God who accept the invitation of salvation, Romans 8 says we receive the Spirit of Adoption as sons (and daughters), and therefore heirs of God, and fellow heirs with Christ. Jesus expanded His family of origin to include a family of faith for all eternity. We are blood-bought relatives and co-heirs with Christ. As His brothers and sisters by faith, we enter into true relationship first with Him, then with one another. True relationship starts with faith in the One who shows us that obedience can be thicker than blood, because the blood of Christ is the only blood with the power to forgive, reconcile, and redeem.

PRAYER

> *Dear Lord,* we desire a faith and an obedience that we do not possess apart from you. Thank You for making a way through Christ to enter into true, authentic relationship with You and then with others. Mercifully prepare us, just as You did Mary, for the journey toward our destiny. In Jesus's name. Amen.

CHAPTER FOURTEEN

Lead Me to the Cross

When Jesus saw his mother standing there beside the disciple he loved, he said to her, "Dear woman, here is your son."

—*John 19:26* NLT

March 5, 2015, began like any other day for my family. My alarm clock woke me, I got ready, then I woke all three children. They got ready, and we managed to pull it all together, pile into the Suburban, and get to school on time. I proceeded to go to work and tackle a never-ending list, and so began our normal, mundane, at-least-it's-almost-spring day. Then my family got the call. That SOS from the crystal waters of the Bahamas would echo in our souls for days, months, and years to come.

My brother Jonathan and his girlfriend had embarked on the adventure of a lifetime, sailing to the Bahamas in January. Jonathan's sights were on South America and beyond, so the trip to the Bahamas was merely a trial run at life on the sea. Judging from their blog and the incredible pictures of crystal waters and never-ending sky, life was good as a captain with his first mate. At least that is how I choose to remember him—happy, free, and doing what he loved with the one he loved.

On the morning of March 5, Jonathan was kite sailing several miles offshore, his sailboat anchored nearby, when something from the water attacked him. Jonathan was conscious and communicating all the way to the rescue vessel, and finally to the ambulance, but the wound in his leg was massive and the blood loss overwhelming. That tragic day my brother of thirty-three years died doing what brought him great joy.

SOS is commonly known as a universal distress call for sailors. Although it is not technically an acronym, it has been equated with the terms "save our ship" and "save our souls." The day my brother died, we received two calls. The first call notified us that his sailboat, Dalila, had sent out an SOS. Someone was injured and in need of medical assistance. The second call informed us that the injured one was Jonathan, and despite all efforts to save him, his soul had passed from this world. For my parents, SOS became their hearts' cry of "save our son," but then they cried, "Dear God, why didn't you save our son?"

The rain that poured from the sky that day as I left the office, leaning on my husband's strength, was no match for the tears our family would shed over the next hours, days, months, and years. Grief was introduced like a slap in the face and a kick in the gut, a guest that was never invited in and may never leave. Grief was now a "frenemy," a friend when you need it to cope and heal, but an enemy who pierces your soul, often without warning. Grief became its own type of SOS to God: "Save my soul, Lord, before this pain becomes the end of me." Dr. Larry Crabb says perseverance is a deep calling. And such is grief. I now understand.

Mary the mother of Jesus was introduced to such grief the day she journeyed with her Son from Jerusalem, where she had dedicated Him to God, all the way to the Place of the Skull, where they would nail Him to a cross. *Save our Son* became the silent cry of her heart. Just imagine Mary as a bystander in the scene that unfolds in John 19.

Beginning in verse one, Pilate had Jesus flogged with a lead-tipped whip. Next, soldiers mocked Him with a crown of thorns and a purple robe, exclaiming, "Hail! King of the Jews!" After questioning Jesus's true identity, Pilate presented Jesus to the masses, causing a crescendo of shouts—first from the leading priests and guards, then from the crowd. "Away with him," they yelled. "Away with him! Crucify him!" (v. 15). Can you imagine the crescendo of shock and fear rising in Mary's heart, bursting forth in tears of helpless desperation as she witnessed a court of human cruelty hand down a sentence of undeserved death? At that moment, the first nail was hammered into her Son's destiny as Pilate turned Jesus over to them to be crucified.

John 19:17–18 (NLT) says, "Carrying the cross by himself, he went to the place called Place of the Skull (in Hebrew, *Golgotha*). There they nailed him to the cross. Two others were crucified with him, one on either side, with Jesus between them." Can you imagine what it must have felt like for Mary to hear the crushing words, "Crucify him," much less follow her Son's bloodstained path to the cross? Perhaps Mary stood in disbelief, paralyzed by fear as the guards loaded a cross on His flesh-torn back. John confirms that a trinity of Marys were present at the cross. Perhaps this community of Marys helped Jesus's mother make her way toward the hardest grief she would ever know. John 19:25–27 (NLT) says,

Standing near the cross were Jesus's mother, and his mother's sister, Mary (the wife of Clopas), and Mary Magdalene. When Jesus saw his mother standing there beside the disciple He loved, He said to her, "Dear woman, here is your son." And he said to this disciple, "Here is your mother." And from then on, this disciple took her into his home.

Pastor Peter Larson wrote in *Prism* magazine (Jan/Feb 2001), "Despite our efforts to keep Him out, God intrudes. The life of Jesus is bracketed by two impossibilities: a virgin's womb and an empty tomb." Yet between these two impossibilities is the harsh reality of the cross. Death on a cross for her not-so-long-ago baby Jesus, whom she laid in a manger, had to be an impossible scene for Mary to bear. She could barely endure this journey, and it was never erased from her mind. For Mary, the death of Jesus was unlike anyone else's experience. Both Jesus and Mary beckon us all to the cross: to know what they knew, and to find hope to live beyond the darkest days.

I cannot imagine what Mary was feeling or thinking in these excruciating moments. Her heart must have shattered more and more with every blow of the lash to her Son's back. I can't imagine the visceral pain she experienced as witness to such human cruelty and gross injustice. As a mother of three, I can't fathom how Mary stood at the foot of the cross in humble obedience to her calling as His mother, destined to lose a Son in order to gain an eternal Savior. I can hardly imagine walking in her footsteps, but I can share with you what it is like to watch a mother and a father lose their son too soon, at the same age as Jesus was when He was crucified on the cross.

While the scene of Jesus dying a criminal's death on the cross is gory and gruesome, there is a beautiful dichotomy at the cross between Mary's silence and Jesus's words. In order to place yourself there at the scene, I invite you to take a moment and reread John 19 as if you are Mary. God had been mercifully preparing Mary for her own journey to the foot of the cross ever since Jesus's conception. What a journey of devotion to Jesus, when perhaps only faith remained.

Jesus spoke several poignant words from the cross: words for those crucifying Him, words to those being crucified beside Him, words to His followers, words to His Father, and words of prophecy. Perhaps some of the most telling and moving words He spoke from the cross were to His mother. "When Jesus saw his mother standing there beside the disciple he loved, he said to her, 'Dear woman, here is your son.' And he said to this disciple, 'Here is your mother'" (Jn. 19:26–27 NLT). In excruciating pain and with His flesh failing, in His last few spoken words and His last few breaths, Christ extended God's hand of mercy and made provision for His mother with the disciple He loved. In His most helpless condition, as He prepared to surrender His own Spirit, and while Love held Him on the cross, Providence stepped in and provided for the ones He held most dear. Providence is defined as God's divine care, guidance, fate, and/or destiny, and Providence always provides and protects.

If Love held Jesus on the cross, then Faith held Mary silent at the foot of the cross. Mary's faith in those moments unleashed God's immediate, gracious provision for both Mary and John. The Scriptures don't tell us if Mary spoke or cried, or even winced as she watched her Son bleed to death, but her silence speaks volumes beyond any words she may have uttered. What do you imagine Mary was feeling, thinking, or enduring in these hours and moments leading up to her Son's death? Perhaps she silently prayed to God a prayer similar to Jesus's: "Father, if you are willing, remove this cup from me; yet not my will, but yours be done" (Lk. 22:42 NASB). In silent submission, after years of merciful preparation for her Son's destiny, Mary accepted God's will and trusted His plan despite the personal cost to her broken heart and silent tears.

Mark Lowery, writer of "Mary Did You Know?" once said at a conference I attended, and I paraphrase: "We know that the gospel is true and that Jesus Christ became sin, who knew no sin. He was beaten, crucified, and died on a cross to save us from sin, death and the grave. We know this to be true *all* because of the silence of His mother at the foot of the cross." Take a minute to ponder the faith of a woman who pondered much and submitted to much more.

How does Mary's silence speak to your heart? Perhaps you have experienced a time when submitting to God's will was the hardest and highest calling you have ever received. There is a saying that "Silence gives consent." In these horrific moments at the cross, Mary allowed God to be God, surrendering herself to His will, accepting her destiny as His mother, and embracing the next steps of grief and sorrow with faith and unconditional trust.

Perhaps this was the day that Mary, while others present at the foot of the cross must have looked away, looked into the face of God, in all His suffering and glory, and lived. The unconditional love of a mother for her Son made room for the unconditional trust in God, who was asking Mary—and is still asking us—to surrender, accept, and embrace Him and His way and just take the next step in faith. Mary's silence (in faith) is the equal to our prayer (in faith), "Lord, whatever it takes." Are we willing to pray, "Lord, whatever it takes"? Do we love and trust Him enough to surrender all?

1 John 5:4–5 (NLT) says, "For every child of God defeats this evil world, and we achieve this victory through our faith. And who can win this battle against the world? Only those who believe that Jesus is the Son of God." Mary was a child of God even before she became a mother. As evidenced by her silence, she knew that Jesus's death on a cross was the will of God. Therefore, Mary believed Jesus to be the Son of God, and *her* faith at the cross becomes *our* victory.

I've heard it said that faith precedes understanding. We don't have to understand to believe, because knowing and understanding are entirely two different things. Did Mary fully understand why her Son was crucified? Perhaps only in part. Mary, the mother of Jesus, was not among the women who arrived at the tomb on the Sunday morning following her Son's crucifixion on Friday afternoon. She was also not listed as one of the women preparing spices and ointments for Jesus's body before and after the Saturday Sabbath to honor Jesus in His death and burial. No, perhaps Mary was somewhere isolated and quiet, suffering from a broken heart, crying and grieving. Mary was grieving her earthly loss because she was yet to fully embrace heaven's gain.

Losing my brother was the hardest thing the Lord has ever asked my parents or me to endure. We sat in disbelief for hours and days, until his girlfriend was able to fly home and sit at my kitchen table and give an eyewitness, first-responder account of her attempt to rescue, save, and ultimately lose the one she adored. Our family, alongside his girlfriend, cried out to God in our pain, asking the most dangerous question: Why? We woke up each day only to realize the harsh reality that life and work and people and traffic and time move on, with or without us. We embodied every emotion, from anger to acceptance, all in our own way and in our own timing. Yet over time and tears, we came to a place of being able to celebrate the life he lived, instead of only grieving the life he'd lost.

We endured what author Sheldon Vanauken penned "a mercy as severe as death" in our own story of faith, tragedy, and triumph. In his book *A Severe Mercy*, Vanauken recalls the intense grief he endured after the death of his wife, yet how he left himself open to what grief could teach him. Grief ultimately taught Vanauken, as well as my family, the merciful love of God.

As each passing day turned into months, and now years, my family and I have witnessed firsthand the arm of mercy that Christ extends from the cross to those who are willing to meet Him there. In order to grieve and grieve well, my family and I had to learn to live out Matthew 16:24: "Let him deny himself and take up his cross and follow me." Daily we are called to give up our own stubborn ways (thoughts and behaviors), take up (accept) our own cross (burdens and trials), and follow Him (wherever He takes us). We have learned to embrace the little reminders of Jonathan, the pictures, the endearing stories of adventure and heroics, even the kayak without a rider launched down the Nantahala in his honor. Grief has slowly transformed into inspiration to live as Jonathan lived: free, present, and ready for where the day takes us.

Providence always provides and protects in ways we least expect and often don't understand. What kind of provision and protection has Jesus extended to you from the cross? For Mary, her worst nightmare became the source of God's greatest provision in Jesus Christ. Jesus's provision for Mary also demonstrates His provision for each one of us, as well as the church body, the people of God. Let Jesus lead you to the cross and allow Him to show you that His provision of salvation is only the beginning of what He can do for you.

PRAYER

Lord, lead us to the cross, where Love and Hope triumph over suffering and death when we put our faith in You, and You alone. In Jesus's name. Amen.

CHAPTER FIFTEEN

From Sorrow to Joy: When Hard Questions Become Powerful Prayers

Prayer doesn't prepare us for the greater work, prayer is the greater work.

—Oswald Chambers

My brother Jonathan was known as Jon Clark by his friends and cohorts in life and work at the Nantahala Outdoor Center (NOC). Following his death, they collaborated and decided to honor his memory and embody his adventurous spirit by making bracelets with the letters WWJCD: "What would Jon Clark do?" It is a question his friends all want to remember to ask themselves when approaching a crossroads of potential adventure and risk, as opposed to a ride on easy street. While Jon Clark knew and respected his personal boundaries in life and relationships, he was known to push the boundary of adventure and risk when it came to whitewater sports.

When I first laid eyes on one of these bracelets, my heart paused. I was temporarily speechless about the gesture. Did it mean to say WWJD (What would Jesus do)? No, it said WWJCD. I asked myself if this was an appropriate way to remember my dear brother, wearing a bracelet with the strikingly similar question of "What would Jesus do?" Was this borderline sacrilegious? This was a question only God could help me sort out in my own heart and mind, and His answer was surprising. God transformed a hard question of remembrance into a powerful prayer. And it is the kind of question we all have to ask ourselves at the crossroads of fear or faith.

What would Jesus do? Perhaps Mary the mother of Jesus was the very first person to ever ask the question, "What would Jesus do?" Especially in the days following His death, when all hope of saving His life had vanished, she found her chasm of grief to be as deep and wide as her love for her Son. We grieve to the extent that we love—a truth both comforting and terrifying. Mary may have awakened on that Saturday morning paralyzed with grief, shaken to her core because she had just lost the Son who showed her the way, the truth, and the life. Without Jesus she was lost. Without Jesus she was confused. Without Jesus she felt void of life. Without Jesus, *we* are like Mary on Saturday morning.

Saturday was the Sabbath, and perhaps God in His mercy gave Mary space and time to mourn, with nothing and no one requiring her attention. The Sabbath is a day of true rest to ponder His Will and His Way. Perhaps for Mary it was a day to wrestle with the hard and often dangerous questions that accompany grief: questions like, "Why God?" "What if?" "Why me?" "Why *my* son?" and "Why Your Son?" Many such questions from those who already believed, but now felt uncertain, echoed throughout the Kidron Valley following Jesus's crucifixion. Questions like the prophet Jeremiah voiced to the God of Israel in Jeremiah 8:18–19 (NLT), "My grief is beyond healing; my heart is broken. Listen to the weeping of my people; it can be heard all across the land. Has the Lord abandoned Jerusalem? the people ask. Is her King no longer there?" Approximately six hundred years later, Mary experienced the heart cry of Israel's weeping prophet, as her own tears poured out on a cross-shaped altar of grief and sacrifice.

Then on Sunday morning, as Mary quite possibly woke with swollen eyes and a sunken heart, afraid to face another day without Joseph and now without Jesus, she must have heard a commotion stirring in the streets of Jerusalem. Scripture doesn't tell us how, or when, or by whom Mary heard the good news of an empty tomb. In fact, following the scene at the cross, the next and last place we find Mary in Scripture is in Acts 1. She was in the upper room, praying with the disciples and others, including women, after the ascension of Christ. That makes several pivotal weeks (forty days to be exact) following Christ's resurrection and leading up to His ascension in which we can only speculate. We can only try to fill in the blanks of Mary's firsthand experience.

After Jesus placed Mary into His beloved disciple's care, perhaps John was the one who gently came to Mary in her grief-stricken state to share the discovery of the empty tomb and the evidence of the risen Messiah. Can you imagine the tug-of-war that took place in Mary's heart between grief and hope, as she began to realize the fullness of God's plan of salvation through Jesus Christ, the now-risen Messiah? I wish Scripture included the reunion of the resurrected Jesus with His mother. However, many of our most intimate and sacred moments in life are meant to remain private between us and God. As she laid eyes on Jesus's nail-scarred hands, I can only imagine Mary breaking out in another Magnificat, praising God for His glorious plan. Once and for all, everyone who believes that Jesus is God's only Son will receive atonement for sin and new life for eternity.

Perhaps the forty days following Jesus's resurrection were a merciful preparation for Mary's final farewell at His ascension. She probably began to understand what Colossians 1:19–20 says: "For God was pleased to have all his fullness dwell in him, and through him to reconcile to himself all things, whether things on earth or things in heaven, by making peace through his blood, shed on the cross." As the storm clouds of grief parted and the Son appeared in all His glory, perhaps Mary fully understood God's plan and purpose through the life, death, and resurrection of Jesus Christ.

Mary's final appearance in Scripture follows the ascension of Christ. She and Jesus's disciples had traveled from the Mount of Olives to the upper room in Jerusalem to pray in one accord for the promised Holy Spirit. "All these with one accord were devoting themselves to prayer, together with the women and Mary the mother of Jesus, and his brothers" (Acts 1:14). Can you imagine what Mary must have prayed as she knelt, surrounded by Jesus's disciples, other women who loved Jesus, and her other sons? Can you fathom the painful but powerful prayer of a mother who had to once again surrender her Son to God's will as He ascended into the clouds?

Perhaps some of the men and women with Mary in the upper room were praying on her behalf, because some prayers are too painful to pray alone. Sometimes we need other believers to intercede with us in faith. Perhaps for Mary it was a *painful* prayer to surrender the life of her Son, yet a *powerful* prayer to live on, with the hope of the Spirit of Christ dwelling in her once again. Without Jesus in the flesh, prayer became Mary's lifeline to the strength and the power through His Spirit to live on in faith. The same is true for every believer.

For any mother or father who loses a child, this is a dark, cold, lengthy and thorny path to tread fully exposed and barefoot. Ironically, grief becomes your only means of protection for at least a while. The weight of initial grief isolates and insulates and presses you down just long enough for you to have time to learn to breathe again. As a sister, I endured the initial dark, hopeless days of grief curled up in bed, asking God the difficult questions and praying painful prayers on behalf of my grief-stricken parents. I watched my parents self-protect, isolate, insulate, and try to breathe each next breath.

During this time I thought of Mary and her Saturday grief and isolation from Jesus, the greatest love and hope she had ever known. Jesus had traveled from her womb to the tomb, perhaps a place she could not muster the strength to visit. During the initial shock of losing a loved one, grief is too fresh and raw for the healing balm of hope to penetrate.

After my brother's death, one of the most painful moments of my life was hearing my brother's girlfriend give her account of my brother's fatal injury and her attempt to save his life. While my father was present and wanted to understand the facts, my stepmother made the decision in her own grief that hearing the details of her son's death was too much for her soul to bear. She respectfully declined the opportunity to hear and know, and visualize and endure yet another painful blow. Although my medical mind sought to know, and wanted to try to understand the reason his injury turned fatal, my stepmom honored her own personal boundaries of heartache. For that, I both respect and admire her decision. To this day, including what I'm sharing here, I am careful not to discuss or share details that may unnecessarily pierce her heart any deeper than Jonathan's death already has.

After watching my parents grieve over the last few years, I have come to believe my stepmom made a wise decision to spare herself the details of her son's death. After enduring the initial, raw days and months of grief, and surviving the dreadful firsts—like the first birthday without her son and the first anniversary of his death—she has arrived at a place of peace and rest. She has accepted God's plan and purpose for her son's death. As my stepmom turned to God through prayer in the midst of her grief and pain, she began to find healing and supernatural strength to face each day and each reminder of her loss. My brother's friends embraced his adventurous spirit with bracelets asking, "What would Jon Clark do?" Similarly, my family began to embrace the hope of celebrating his life in the midst of grieving his death.

Perhaps just as Mary was given new life and hope in Christ when the Holy Spirit came over her in her grief, my family and I were given a new hope by celebrating my brother's adventurous spirit following his death. Jon Clark possessed many Christlike characteristics, including a gentle and quiet, but fearless spirit that brought the best out in people and challenged them to dig deeper within themselves. He was a man of few words who lived out a simple, childlike faith, often advocating for those who could not help themselves.

Just as the life of Christ beckons the question, "What would Jesus do?" so my brother's life seemed to evoke a similar question for his friends and family: "What would Jon Clark do?" I discovered it isn't a wrong or sacrilegious question to ask. It's a hard question that God transformed into a powerful prayer, because only God, through the power of the Holy Spirit, can guide me through life without the presence and wisdom of my brother, as I care for my parents.

Isaiah 61:3 (NLT) says, "To all who mourn in Israel, he will give a crown of beauty for ashes, a joyous blessing instead of mourning, festive praise instead of despair. In their righteousness, they will be like great oaks that the Lord has planted for his own glory." For those who have lost loved ones, our crown of beauty, blessing, and praise will ultimately be fulfilled in heaven when we reunite with those we've lost for a time. For the righteous who live by faith, sorrow and suffering in this life will be transformed into eternal joy when we meet Jesus face to face in all His glory. "For through the Spirit, by faith, we ourselves eagerly wait for the hope of righteousness. For in Christ Jesus neither circumcision nor uncircumcision counts for anything, but only faith working through love" (Gal. 5:5–6).

In this life, we are promised joy mixed with pain, as there is no quota on suffering; however, abundant life is offered through faith in Jesus Christ. During the tough times in life, when it seems only faith remains, faith alone keeps us connected to the ultimate Source of hope and love.

Just as prayer became Mary's lifeline to Jesus in the upper room, prayer remains one of the most powerful sources of hope, strength, love, and peace for believers. As Oswald Chambers wrote in *My Utmost for His Highest*, "Prayer doesn't prepare us for the greater work, prayer *is* the greater work." It requires faith to pray, and during the times when only faith remains, prayer is our lifeline to Jesus. A prayer, offered and lifted up in faith to the One who gives us faith, reconnects us to Hope and Love in the Person of Jesus Christ. We are made for relationship with Jesus. Therefore, Faith, Hope, and Love is a Person—not just a feeling, or a product of your circumstances and performance in life. Prayer is the greater work, because it helps us fully depend on Jesus as the Way, the Truth, and the Life.

Throughout my journey of faith, the hard questions have become some of the most powerful prayers. Questions like, "Why me?" when I was struggling with my parents' divorce, or battling with bulimia, became prayers like, "Why not me, Lord?" that led to forgiveness and healing. Difficult questions like, "Why did I have to get injured?" when I was suffering from depression, became powerful prayers such as, "May this injury lead me to a new calling all for your glory." This later led me into the profession of physical therapy.

Painful questions like, "Would I still love you, Lord, if my son had drowned?" changed into life-changing prayers such as, "Help me surrender into your grace," as I began experiencing the sacrificial love of God. And grief-laden questions like, "Why did my brother have to die so young?" transformed into prayers of gratitude and thanksgiving for the adventure-filled life he had lived.

Perhaps you have some of your own hard questions regarding events or circumstances in your life. Take some time to reflect and write down those difficult questions. Then, through the power of the Holy Spirit, ask God to help you transform your hard questions into powerful prayers. Perhaps the times during which Mary pondered and treasured her thoughts and questions ultimately became prayers, as she obediently lived out her calling. Looking back on Mary's life and journey of faith from the manger to the cross, have you found parallels in your own life and your journey of faith? How has Mary's journey of faith encouraged or inspired you? What has Mary's life revealed to you about God?

My prayer is that your faith in Jesus Christ has been renewed or strengthened. During the times in life when only faith remains, know that God has not forsaken you. Be assured that faith will lead you to the ultimate source of Hope and Love. When only faith remains, and it is your last hope of ever experiencing the love of God, don't give up. Jesus alone has the power to turn your questions into prayers and your sorrow into joy, as you hold fast to faith.

PRAYER

Dear Lord, we are all on a journey of faith, just with different details and circumstances. May our journey, like Mary's, ultimately lead us to the cross and beyond, all by faith. And during the times in life when only faith remains, help us to hold fast to faith, wait patiently in prayer, and eagerly anticipate the greatest source of Hope and Love in the Person of Jesus Christ. In His Holy Name. Amen.

Order Information

To order additional copies of this book, please visit
www.redemption-press.com.
Also available on Amazon.com and BarnesandNoble.com
Or by calling toll free 1-844-2REDEEM.